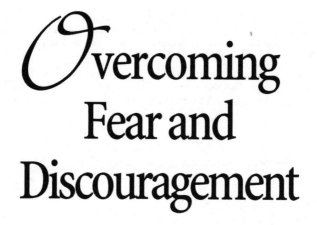

Overcoming
Fear and
Discouragement

KAY ARTHUR
DAVID LAWSON
BOB VEREEN

HARVEST HOUSE™ PUBLISHERS

EUGENE, OREGON

Contents

ରରରର

The New Inductive Study Series
OVERCOMING FEAR AND DISCOURAGEMENT

Copyright © 1999 by Precept Ministries International
Published by Harvest House Publishers
Eugene, Oregon 97402

Library of Congress Cataloging-in-Publication Data
Arthur, Kay, 1933–
    Overcoming fear and discouragement / Kay Arthur, David Lawson, and Bob Vereen
        p. cm. — (The new inductive study series)
    ISBN 0-7369-0810-2
    1. Bible. O.T. Ezra—Study and teaching 2. Bible. O.T. Nehemiah—Study and
    teaching. 3. Bible. O.T. Esther—Study and teaching. I. Title. II. Series: Arthur, Kay,
    1933–   New inductive study series.
BS1355.5.A78 1999
222'.7'0071—dc21   99-21976
                                                                                        CIP

Printed in the United States of America.

        02 03 04 05 06 07 08 09 10 / BP-CF / 10 9 8 7 6 5 4 3 2 1

WHAT AM I DOING?

You are about to begin a study which will revolutionize not only your approach to the Word of God, but also your understanding and comprehension of the Word. This is the consistent testimony of those who are using this series.

The New Inductive Study Series is the first series of its kind in that it is a 15- to 25-minute daily study that takes you systematically through the Bible, book by book, teaching you to observe the text and see for yourself what it says. The more you learn to carefully observe the text and to familiarize yourself with the context in which specific texts are presented, the closer you will come to an accurate and unbiased interpretation of God's Word. This, in turn, will help you correctly apply the truth of God's Word—and to find yourself transformed in the process.

As you go through this series, remember that it is an inductive survey of the various books of the Bible. The purpose of this series is to help you get a comprehensive overview of the whole counsel of God so that you will be better able to let Scripture interpret Scripture and to understand truth in the context of the Bible, book by book and in its entirety.

If you desire to expand and sharpen your study skills, we would like to recommend two things. One, purchase the book *How to Study Your Bible* by Kay Arthur. Two, attend a Precept Ministries Institute of Training.

The Institutes are conducted throughout the United States, Canada, and in a number of other countries. You can attend classes of various lengths—from two hours to five full days, depending on the courses you elect to take. Whatever your choices, you will join the thousands who are absolutely awed at the way God has enriched their relationship with Him and deepened their understanding of His Word. For more information on the Precept Ministries Institute of Training, call our Information Department at (800) 763-8280, visit our website at www.precept.org, or fill out and mail the response card at the back of this book.

We don't know if you have ever used one of the books in our New Inductive Study Series before, so let us acknowledge that reading directions is sometimes difficult and hardly ever enjoyable! Most often, you just want to get started. Only if all else fails are you ready to tackle the instructions! We understand—we're not into details, either. But read "How to Get Started" before you begin. This is a vital part of getting started on the right foot! The pages are few...and they will help you immensely.

*H*OW TO *G*ET *S*TARTED...

FIRST

As you study the books of Ezra, Nehemiah, and Esther, you will need four things in addition to this book:

1. A Bible you are willing to mark in. Marking is essential because it is an integral part of the learning process and will help you remember and retain what you learned. An ideal Bible for this purpose is *The New Inductive Study Bible (NISB)*. The *NISB,* available in the NAS version, comes in a single-column text format with larger, easy-to-read type, and is ideal for marking. The page margins are wide and blank for note taking.

The *NISB* is unique among all study Bibles in that it has instructions for studying each book of the Bible, but it does not contain any commentary on the text. The *NISB* isn't compiled from any particular theological stance since its purpose is to teach you how to discern truth for yourself through the inductive method of study. Inductive Bible study simply means that the Bible itself is one's primary source for study. (The various charts and maps that you will find in this study guide are taken from the *NISB.*) Whatever Bible you use, just know you will need to mark in it, which brings us to the second item you will need.

2. A fine-point, four-color ballpoint pen or various colored fine-point pens (such as Micron pens) for writing in your Bible. The Micron pens are best for this purpose. Office supply stores should have these.

3. Colored pencils or an eight-color Pentel pencil.

4. A composition notebook or loose-leaf notebook for working on your assignments and recording your insights.

SECOND

1. As you study this book, you'll find specific instructions for each day's study. The study should take you between 15 and 25 minutes a day. However, just know that the more time you can give to this study, the greater the spiritual dividends, and the greater your intimacy with the Word of God and the God of the Word. If you are doing this study within the framework of a class and you find the lessons too heavy, simply do what you can. To do a little is better than to do nothing. Don't be an all-or-nothing person when it comes to Bible study.

As a word of warning, you need to be aware that anytime you get into the Word of God, you enter into more intensive warfare with the devil (our enemy). Why? Every piece of the Christian's armor is related to the Word of God. And the enemy doesn't want you prepared for battle. Thus, the warfare! Remember that our one and only offensive weapon is the sword of the Spirit, which is the Word of God, and it is enough to fell the enemy.

To study or not to study is a matter of choice first, discipline second. It's a matter of the heart. On what or whom are you setting your heart? Get armed for war! And remember, victory is certain.

2. As you read each chapter, train yourself to think through the content of the text by asking the "5 W's and an

H": who, what, when, where, why, and how. Posing questions like these and searching out the answers helps you see exactly what the Word of God is saying. When you interrogate the text with the 5 W's and an H, you ask questions like these:

   a. **Who** are the main characters?
   b. **What** is the chapter about?
   c. **When** does this event or teaching take place?
   d. **Where** does this occur?
   e. **Why** is this being done or said?
   f. **How** did this happen?

3. The "when" of events or teachings is very important and should be marked in an easily recognizable way in your Bible. We do this by putting a clock (like the one shown here) ⏰ in the margin of our Bibles beside the verse where the time phrase occurs. Or you may want to underline references to time in one specific color. As a reminder, note on your key-word bookmark (which is explained next in this section) how you are going to mark time references in each chapter.

4. You will be told about certain key words that you should mark throughout this study. This is the purpose of the colored pencils and the colored pen. While this may seem a little time-consuming, you will discover that it is a valuable learning tool. If you will develop the habit of marking your Bible, you will find it will make a significant difference in the effectiveness of your study and in how much you retain as a result of your study.

A **key word** is an important word that is used by the author repeatedly in order to convey his message to his reader. Certain key words will show up throughout the book, while other key words will be concentrated in specific chapters or segments of the book. When you mark a key word, you should also mark its synonyms (words that have the same meaning in a particular context) and any pronouns *(he, his, she, her, it, we, they, us, our, you, their, them)* in the same way you have marked the key word. Because some people have requested them, we will give you various ideas and suggestions in your daily assignments for how you can mark different key words.

Marking words for easy identification can be done by colors, symbols, or a combination of colors and symbols. However, colors are easier to distinguish than symbols. If you use symbols, we suggest you keep them very simple. For example, one of the key words in Esther is *Jew*. You could draw a star of David like this over Jew and color it blue. If a symbol is used in marking a key word, it is best for the symbol to somehow convey the meaning of the word.

As you begin this new venture, we recommend that you devise a color-coding system for marking key words that you decide to mark throughout your Bible. Then, when you glance at the pages of your Bible, you will have instant recognition of the words.

In marking the members of the Godhead *(which we do not always mark),* we use a triangle to represent the Father. We then color it yellow. Then, playing off the triangle, we mark the Son this way: Jesus, and the Holy Spirit this way: Spirit. We find that when you mark every reference to God and Jesus, your Bible becomes cluttered. However, since the Spirit is mentioned less and because many people do not have a thorough biblical understanding of the Holy Spirit, it is good to mark the references to the Spirit of God. Of course, mostly you will see references to God in the Old

Testament, but we wanted you to know what we do when we are studying other books of the Bible.

When you start marking key words, it is easy to forget how you are marking them. You may wish to use the bottom portion of the perforated card in the back of this book to write key words on. Mark the words the way you plan to mark them in your Bible and then use the card as a bookmark. Make one bookmark for words you are marking throughout your Bible, and a different one for any specific book of the Bible you are studying. Or record your marking system for the words you plan to mark throughout your Bible on a blank page in your Bible.

5. Because locations are important in historical books and they tell you "where," you will find it helpful to mark locations in a distinguishable way in your study. Try double-underlining every reference to a location in green (grass and trees are green!). We suggest that you make a note on your key-word bookmark to mark locations. A map is included in this study so you can look up the locations mentioned in Ezra, Nehemiah, and Esther in order to put yourself into context geographically.

6. Charts called EZRA AT A GLANCE, NEHEMIAH AT A GLANCE, and ESTHER AT A GLANCE are located at the end of each book. When you complete your study of each chapter of these books, record the main theme of that chapter on the appropriate chart. A chapter theme is a brief description or summary of the main theme or predominant subject, teaching, or event covered in that chapter.

When stating chapter themes, it is best to use words found within the text itself and to be as brief as possible. Make sure that you do them in such a way as to distinguish one chapter from another. Doing this will help you to remember what each chapter is about. In addition, it will provide you with a ready reference if you desire to find something in the book rather quickly and without a lot of page turning.

If you develop the habit of filling out the AT A GLANCE charts as you progress through the study, you will have a complete synopsis of the book when you finish. If you have a *New Inductive Study Bible,* you will find the same charts in your Bible. If you record your chapter themes on the charts in your Bible and on the designated line at the head of each chapter in the text, you'll always have a quick synopsis of the chapter and the book.

7. Begin your study with prayer. Don't start without it. Why? Well, although you are doing your part to handle the Word of God accurately, remember that the Bible is a divinely inspired book. The words you are reading are absolute truth, given to you by God so that you can know Him and His ways more intimately. These truths are divinely understood.

> For to us God revealed them through the Spirit; for the Spirit searches all things, even the depths of God. For who among men knows the thoughts of a man except the spirit of the man which is in him? Even so the thoughts of God no one knows except the Spirit of God (1 Corinthians 2:10,11).

This is why you need to pray. Simply tell God you want to understand His Word so you can live accordingly. Nothing pleases Him more than obedience—honoring Him as God—as you are about to see.

8. Each day, when you finish your lesson, take some time to think about what you read, what you saw with your own eyes. Ask your heavenly Father how you can apply

these insights, principles, precepts, and commands to your own life. At times, depending on how God speaks to you through His Word, you might want to record these "Lessons for Life" in the margin of your Bible next to the text you have studied. Simply put "LFL" in the margin of your Bible, then, as briefly as possible, record the lesson for life that you want to remember. You can also make the note "LFL" on your key-word bookmark as a reminder to look for these when you study. You will find them encouraging...sometimes convicting...when you come across them again, and they will be a reminder of what God has shown you from His Word.

THIRD

This study is designed so that you have an assignment for every day of the week. This puts you where you should be—in the Word of God on a daily basis, grasping, systematizing, and utilizing truth. It's revolutionary!

If you will do your study daily, you will find it more profitable than doing a week's study in one sitting. Pacing yourself this way allows time for thinking through what you learn on a daily basis. However, whatever it takes to get it done, do it!

The seventh day of each week has several different features that differ from the other six days. These features are designed to aid in one-on-one discipleship, group discussions, and Sunday school classes. However, they are also profitable even if you are studying this book by yourself.

The "seventh" day is whatever day in the week you choose to think about and/or discuss your week's study. On this day, you will find a verse or two for you to memorize and thus STORE IN YOUR HEART. This will help you focus on a major truth or truths covered in your study that week.

To assist those using the material for discipleship, family devotions, or in a Sunday school class or a group Bible study, there are QUESTIONS FOR DISCUSSION OR INDIVIDUAL STUDY. Whatever your situation, seeking to answer these questions will help you reason through some key issues in the study.

If you are using the study in a group setting, make sure the answers given are supported from the Bible text itself. This practice will help ensure that you are handling the Word of God accurately. As you learn to see what the text says, you will find that the Bible explains itself.

Always examine your insights by carefully observing the text to see what it *says*. Then, before you decide what the passage of Scripture *means,* make sure you interpret it in light of its context. Context is what goes with the text… the Scriptures preceding and following what is written. Scripture will never contradict Scripture. If it ever seems to contradict the rest of the Word of God, you can be certain that something is being taken out of context. If you come to a passage that is difficult to understand, reserve your interpretations for a time when you can study the passage in greater depth.

Your discussion time should cause you to see how to apply these truths to your own life. What are you now going to embrace as truth? How are you going to order your life? Are you going to not only know these truths but live accordingly?

The purpose of a THOUGHT FOR THE WEEK is to help you apply what you've learned. We've done this for your edification. In this, a little of our theology will inevitably come to the surface; however, we don't ask that you always agree with us. Rather, think through what is said in light of the context of the Word of God. You can determine how valuable it is.

Remember, books in The New Inductive Study Series are survey courses. If you want to do a more in-depth study of a particular book of the Bible, we suggest you do a Precept Upon Precept Bible study course on that book. The Precept studies are awesome but require five hours of personal study a week.

*E*ZRA

REBUILDING THE TEMPLE AND RESTORING THE PEOPLE

∾∾∾∾

Ezra is one of the most encouraging books of the entire Bible. In your study of this book, you will see not only God's hand clearly moving in the affairs of men as He lovingly, fairly, and justly performs His purpose, but also how man responds to God's leading and instructions.

You will see God, through His prophets, announcing His future plans hundreds of years in advance; predicting the reigns of kings and kingdoms even before they exist; pre-declaring a precise time schedule that is kept to the very minute; and stirring the hearts of all kinds of people in order to accomplish His will.

In this study, you'll be warned of the penalties that result from disobedience. You'll be encouraged by the lifestyles of those who know His Word and keep it. You'll be comforted by the overwhelming evidence that God continues to work mightily among His creation, regardless of man's responses. And at the same time, you'll be challenged to study His Word, learn His commandments, listen to His voice, and walk in His ways.

On the surface, Ezra appears to be a book about obedience—man's responsibility—but it has a deeper message about the unwavering faithfulness of a sovereign God whose commitment and compassion for His people never changes. His heart is to have an intimate relationship with His people—those who believe in Him. If that relationship is broken by our rebellion against His will, His passion is for the restoration of that relationship!

Ezra was a man who "had set his heart to study the law of the LORD and to practice *it*, and to teach *His* statutes and ordinances in Israel" (Ezra 7:10). Ezra's passion for knowing God caused even the nonbelievers of his day to recognize that "the good hand of his God *was* upon him" (Ezra 7:9). He understood the absolute necessity for man to know the Word of God and to respond appropriately to its commands. Ezra stated it this way: "The hand of our God is favorably disposed to all those who seek Him, but His power and His anger are against those who forsake Him" (Ezra 8:22b).

When we seek Him, He is favorably disposed. When we forsake Him, His power and anger are against us. Yes, He is there moving and working on our behalf. And yes, what we know and what we do does make a difference. Let's begin seeking Him through our study of the book of Ezra. Come study with me and experience His favor.

DOES IT REALLY MATTER WHAT CHOICE I MAKE?

ᕙᕗᕙᕗ

Have you ever made a bad decision and felt like God had distanced Himself from you because of that incorrect choice? Have you ever wanted to just give up? To quit? Have you ever thought it would be impossible to get it all back together again?

Is there any hope? Any way out? Can your relationship with God and others be restored? Will God forgive you? Does God still want to have an intimate relationship with you?

God's answer to all of these questions is a resounding "Yes!"

DAY ONE

Read Ezra chapter 1, asking the "5 W's and an H" kinds of questions. (You were instructed how to do this in the "How to Get Started" section on page 8. If you have not read that section, stop and do so now. It will be very helpful to you as you complete the daily assignments.)

You may have asked some questions such as the following:

   ~ **Who** is Cyrus, king of Persia?

∾ **Who** is Jeremiah?

∾ **What** did Jeremiah say that is now being fulfilled by Cyrus?

∾ **What** "house" is God referring to that He has appointed Cyrus to rebuild for Him?

∾ **Why** were all the articles from the house of the Lord carried away from Jerusalem and put in the house of Nebuchadnezzar's gods?

∾ **Who** is Nebuchadnezzar?

∾ **Who** were the exiles? **Why** were they exiled?

∾ **Who** sent them into exile? **When** did they go into exile? **How** long were they to be in exile?

Since the answers to some of these questions are not found in the text of Ezra itself, we will look for them in other books of the Bible. Discovering these answers will help us establish the historical setting in which the book of Ezra was written. All of your assignments this week are designed to help you lay a solid historical foundation not only for Ezra, but also for your future studies in the books of Nehemiah and Esther.

Let's complete today's time together by reviewing some basic biblical history that will help you understand the background of this book. This background will prove very helpful in understanding Ezra. We will clearly see why the Israelites went into captivity.

Let's begin by seeing how the nation of Israel, the people who are in exile, came into being. First of all, God chose a man named Abram (later called Abraham) and promised him three things:

1) To give him a land (often referred to as "the Promised Land" and later to be called "Israel")

2) To make him a great nation (later to be called the nation of Israel)

3) To give him a seed (Jesus Christ—Galatians 3:16) through whom all the families of the earth would be blessed (Genesis 12:1-3)

Abraham had a son named Isaac who had a son named Jacob. God changed Jacob's name to "Israel." Israel (the person from whom the land and the nation derived its name) had 12 sons who became the "12 tribes of Israel."

Because of a famine in the land, the nation of Israel ended up in Egypt, in slavery to a pharaoh. God chose Moses to lead the children of Israel out of that bondage of slavery (see the book of Exodus) and eventually took the Israelites into the Promised Land under the leadership of Joshua (see the book of Joshua). While en route to the Promised Land, God gave Moses the Ten Commandments on Mount Sinai (Exodus 20). Later, He gave them some other laws, ordinances, and statutes that were designed to help them live their daily lives as a chosen nation for God (the books of Exodus, Leviticus, and Numbers).

During the time of Moses, God instructed him to build a portable tabernacle where the people could worship Him. God would also manifest His presence among the people in the form of a Shekinah glory cloud by day and a pillar of fire by night. That cloud of glory would come down and rest or reside in the Holy of Holies section, which was a part of this tabernacle worship facility.

Many years later, the nation of Israel decided they wanted a king like all the other nations around them. God granted their request and gave them a king named Saul (1 Samuel 10). When Saul died, David became the king of all Israel (2 Samuel 2).

David wanted to replace the tabernacle with a more permanent place of worship, a "house for God." He wanted to build a temple in Jerusalem, the capital of the nation of Israel. God would not allow David to build Him a temple, but allowed David's son Solomon to do it (2 Samuel 7). Solomon completed the construction of the temple in 959 B.C. Then in 931 B.C., Solomon died and the united kingdom of Israel split into two kingdoms, the Northern and the Southern Kingdoms, over a dispute about taxation. The Northern Kingdom (Israel) was comprised of ten of the tribes of Israel, and the Southern Kingdom (Judah) had two tribes.

Look at the chart entitled ISRAEL'S DIVISION AND CAPTIVITY (page 25). Beginning with the date 931 B.C., locate these dates so that you may become familiar with this chart. This will help you understand Israel's history in light of the book of Ezra.

Notice on the chart that the Northern Kingdom of Israel was taken into Assyrian captivity in 722 B.C. For centuries God had pleaded with the Northern Kingdom to turn from their idolatry and immorality, but they would not listen to His messengers. They made a choice which left God with no other choice but to punish them for their disobedience. Assyrian captivity was the consequence of their sin.

Now notice on the chart that the Southern Kingdom of Judah followed in the footsteps of its sister and was taken into Babylonian captivity. This captivity, however, was in three distinct sieges. The first siege was in 605 B.C., the second in 597 B.C., and the third in 586 B.C. Also notice on the chart that the captivity was to last 70 years beginning in

Israel's Division and Captivity

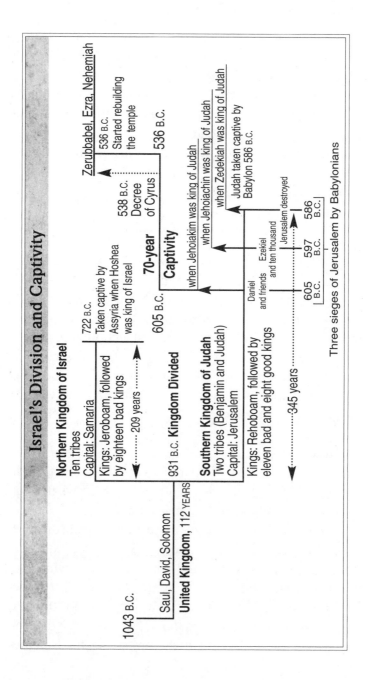

605 B.C., the time of the first siege. You will also see that Jerusalem was totally destroyed in 586 B.C., including the temple that Solomon had built and completed in 959 B.C.

What did the Southern Kingdom do that caused God to allow it to be taken into captivity by the Babylonians? Was it because of idolatry and immorality like the Northern Kingdom? Or was it for other reasons? We will look at that tomorrow.

DAY TWO

Today we will continue to look at the historical setting for the book of Ezra. Read Leviticus 25:1-7. This is one of the many ordinances or statutes that God set before the children of Israel. In your notebook, as briefly as possible, record the main points of God's instruction according to this ordinance. (See the "How to Get Started" section for an explanation of the notebook. It would be good to go back and read this section if you have skipped over it. It contains vital information that you'll need to benefit from this study.)

Now read Leviticus 26:27-35. Record in your notebook what God said He would do to the sons of Israel if they did not obey Him. Be sure to include in your list what would happen to their land and to their sanctuaries.

According to the passage you just read, disobedience to the clear instructions of God has severe consequences. Read Leviticus 26:40-45 and make a list of what God wanted the punishment to do in their hearts and attitudes. Pay particular attention to the long-range commitment to His people that God clearly states in this passage. Note what He says He will not do to His chosen people, the Israelites.

All the facts that you've just observed from these three passages will help you understand what the children of Israel had done wrong and why God had to discipline them. However, we have to gather some more information to make the picture totally clear. Tomorrow we will lay a few more foundation stones in this historical background.

DAY THREE

Read Jeremiah 25:1-12. Jeremiah was a prophet of God during the time when the Southern Kingdom was taken into captivity by Nebuchadnezzar, king of Babylon. As you read these verses, underline the phrase *you have not listened*[1] with a red pen. (If you don't have a red one, use any color.) Also, make a list of the truths you learn from these verses. Make sure that you answer the following questions in your list:

∾ Did the sons of Israel listen to Jeremiah? Did they obey what God had said through him?

∾ Whom did God say He would send against them to destroy them and make their land desolate?

∾ According to verse 9, how did God describe Nebuchadnezzar, the king of Babylon?

∾ What purpose was Nebuchadnezzar accomplishing for God?

∾ How long would the children of Israel serve the king of Babylon?

∾ When the end of the captivity came, what did God say He would do to the king of Babylon?

DAY FOUR

We've seen what law the Israelites failed to obey. We've seen what punishment God was forced to invoke. And we have seen whom God was going to use to discipline His chosen people. Now today let's see how God's servant, Nebuchadnezzar, executed the judgment of God.

Read 2 Chronicles 36:11-21. In your notebook, record the answers to the following:

    ∾ What do you learn about God from this passage?

    ∾ What do you learn about Zedekiah, the king, all the officials of the priests, and the people?

    ∾ What happened to the house of God, to all its articles, and to the wall of Jerusalem?

    ∾ What happened to those who escaped the sword?

DAY FIVE

Obviously the children of Israel had disobeyed many of God's ordinances, statutes, and laws, but specifically they had disobeyed the one regarding the sabbath rest for the land. For 490 years they had not allowed the land to rest every seventh year, thus the accumulated time of rest due the land was 70 years. God would send His people into Babylonian captivity to collect that which was due. But what would happen when the 70 years were over? What would God do then?

Today, read Jeremiah 29:1-14. In your notebook, make a list of God's promises from these verses and answer the following:

∿ What does He promise for those who seek Him?

∿ Is He through with the children of Israel?

∿ What does He tell them to do even in the midst of their time of punishment?

∿ Does He have a future plan for them?

∿ Once the punishment for sin is complete, what is God's desire for His children?

Now then, think about each of these questions and apply it personally to your own relationship with God. For example, what does God promise you if you seek Him? If you do sin and disobey God, is He through with you? Are you to pray to Him in the midst of your chastisement? Does He leave you during this time of punishment? Does God have a future plan for you? Is restoration His desire for you?

In light of what you have learned from the Word of God, if you sin, is it over? Finished? What is your part?

DAY SIX

Today, read Isaiah 44:24–45:7. Mark every reference to Cyrus in a distinctive way by drawing a circle around his name and any pronoun that refers to him. Observe what you learn about him. What would Cyrus do? Make a list of these facts in your notebook.

Isaiah spoke this prophecy regarding Cyrus 175 years before Cyrus was even born! God was raising up another servant to perform His will in the history of man! In 539 B.C. Cyrus, king of Persia, and Darius the Mede, conquered Nebuchadnezzar, king of Babylon, and set the stage for the release of the children of Israel.

With all the information you gained this week about the historical setting, read 2 Chronicles 36:22,23 and Ezra 1:1-4. Now you can see that Ezra is a continuation of the story about the children of Israel, God's chosen people.

To end today's assignment and this week's homework, you need to do one more thing. Go back to Day One and review the questions that came out of Ezra chapter 1 to see if you answered them all. Review your lists in your notebook for the answers.

DAY SEVEN

 Store in your heart: Jeremiah 29:11.

Read and discuss: Ezra 1; Leviticus 25:1-7; 26:27-35, 40-43; Jeremiah 29:10-14; Isaiah 44:24–45:7.

QUESTIONS FOR DISCUSSION OR INDIVIDUAL STUDY

∽ Who took the Northern Kingdom into captivity? What year did that occur?

∽ What were the dates of the three stages of the Babylonian captivity?

∽ How long did the Babylonian captivity last? Under what siege did the time of captivity begin?

∽ In Leviticus 25:1-7, what did God tell the children of Israel to do with the land they were promised and were about to enter?

∽ According to Leviticus 26:27-35, what did God say He would do if the children of Israel disobeyed this ordinance? What will God do to you if you disobey His ordinances?

∞ According to Jeremiah, how long would the captivity last? What would God do at the end of this period of time?

∞ Did God fulfill Jeremiah's prophecy regarding the destruction of Jerusalem?

∞ What did you learn about the character of God from Leviticus 26:40-43? What must the people of Judah do for the sin of disobedience? What must you do if you sin?

∞ From Jeremiah 29:10-14, what did God promise the children of Israel He would do at the end of the 70 years of captivity? What kind of plans does God have for His children? In these verses God promises that when they call to Him, He will "listen" to them. How does this compare to what they would not do when God sent His prophets? Are you listening to God?

∞ When you read Isaiah 44:24–45:7, what did you learn about Cyrus? When was this prophecy given to Isaiah? When did Cyrus, king of Persia, conquer Babylon? How many years are between those two events?

∞ According to Ezra chapter 1, did God do what He said He would do, when He said He would do it?

∞ What are the consequences of disobedience?

∞ Does God discipline those who disobey? Is His discipline always immediately after the act of disobedience?

∞ Does God still discipline His followers who disobey? Whom could He use in His discipline? Believers? Unbelievers? Both?

THOUGHT FOR THE WEEK

God has given us the Bible so that we may know His commandments, statutes, ordinances, and laws. If we know His Word, we can obey it! The more we know and understand His principles and precepts, the more likely we will be to make the right choices. Our responsibility is to know His Word, choose to trust Him in what He says, and choose to obey what He tells us to do.

God has also given us the Holy Spirit to lead us, guide us, and teach us all things. God has given us everything we need in order for us to know what He wants us to do, to think, and to say. Our problem is that sometimes we just make bad decisions. Sometimes it's because we don't know any better. Sometimes it's because we just want to do what's right in our own eyes. We know what to do, but we just choose not to do it. Sometimes we just don't "listen" to His voice or to those messengers He sends our way.

God will go to great lengths to bring us back to the point of obedience. Sometimes He uses unbelievers to accomplish His will. He loves us enough to create and destroy kings and kingdoms and even move us from place to place, if that is what it takes to get us to listen. He faithfully does His part. He desires fellowship with us...whatever the cost on our part or His. His desire is that we confess our sin, change our mind about what we have done, turn from that type of behavior, and return to a life of obedience. Even when we've made a bad choice, we can still make the right choice.

RELEASED TO RETURN

God had promised to punish for disobedience, to restore when restitution had been achieved, and to deliver the children of Israel from the Babylonian captivity, the yoke of His chastisement. He had spoken through His messenger Isaiah about this promise approximately 150 years before that deliverance would occur.

Seventy years of captivity had been promised, but not one second more than 70 years would be allowed. Just as He promised, the time had come...the time to go home. Now He would begin restoring His people to a full, intimate relationship with Him.

DAY ONE

Begin your study this week by reading Ezra 1:1-4. These four verses make up the first of seven letters found in the book of Ezra. As you read this letter, mark in a distinctive manner the word *house* [2] (referring to the house of God). I usually use a purple pen and a symbol that looks like a house (like this: house) over each reference. In your notebook, begin making a list of what you learn about THE HOUSE OF GOD. Be sure to leave some space so that you can add to this list as you go through the rest of the book. It is mentioned in every chapter and, therefore, is considered a "key word" of this book. Key words are simply words that are repeated over and over again in a book. This repetition usually means it is an important subject that is being discussed.

Read these verses again, but this time mark each mention of *Jerusalem.* I use a green pen (green for grass, trees) and put a double underline under all the locations in the Bible so I can quickly see where the event is happening, where the person is going, where the person is from, etc.

In your notebook, under the title THE FIRST LETTER OF EZRA, record just the main points of this letter. You may want to ask some 5 W's and an H questions such as the following:

 ∾ Who wrote the letter? To whom did he write it?

 ∾ According to Ezra, why was Cyrus doing what he was doing (verse 1)?

 ∾ According to Cyrus' perspective, why was he doing what he was doing (verse 2)?

 ∾ When did he write the letter? (Use words from the text.)

 ∾ What were the survivors instructed to do (verses 3,4)?

DAY TWO

Today read Ezra 1:5-11. Again, mark every reference to the *house of the LORD.*[3]

According to verse 5, what did God do to the people to cause them to want to return? Now, look back at verse 1. What did God do to Cyrus? What will God do if He wants you, or a king, to do something? What was it that He wanted the children of Israel to do when they returned to Jerusalem?

Read these verses once again and, in your notebook, make a list of what the people gave to those returning to Jerusalem. Also, make a list of what Cyrus gave to them. Can you imagine how all of this would be transported back to Jerusalem?

Finally, record the main theme of chapter 1 on the EZRA AT A GLANCE chart on page 66. A theme is simply the main idea, point, or teaching the author is trying to get across in the chapter. What do you think is the main point of chapter 1? Record it on the line for chapter 1. When this chart is completed, you will be able to see the main subjects or teachings found in the entire book of Ezra, chapter by chapter. Also, add any other information to the chart that you've learned up to this point.

DAY THREE

Often in the Bible there are lists of names. There are four such lists in the book of Ezra. Many times these are glanced at but not truly read. However, as part of your assignment today, read Ezra 2:1-67. As you read through this list of names, underline the various "groups" of exiles who were returning. For example, the first group mentioned is found in verses 2-39, *the men of the people of Israel;* and then in verse 40, *the Levites;* verse 41, *the singers,* etc.

As you read verses 68-70, ask the who, what, where, when, why, and how questions. Make sure you discover the answers to questions such as: Where did all the exiles reside upon their return? What else did the exiles give toward the rebuilding of the temple?

Again, as you did with chapter 1, summarize chapter 2 and record a brief summary statement that expresses the main theme on your EZRA AT A GLANCE chart on page 66.

DAY FOUR

For the remainder of the week you will spend your time in the third chapter of Ezra. Read through this short chapter and mark every reference to *house* (include *temple*). Add what you learn to your list in your notebook.

References to time are very important, especially when you are trying to establish the chronological sequence of events. It is imperative to understand when the events related to the temple occur.

Read chapter 3 again. This time look for time references. For example, a specific day, month, or year may be mentioned. Mark these references in a specific way, perhaps using the symbol of a clock like you see here ⏰ . In your notebook, list the time references and the events that occurred during each time period.

If you didn't mark the Feast of Booths (also called the Feast of Tabernacles) the same way you did the other references to time, go back and mark it now. The Feast of Tabernacles was a feast celebrating the deliverance of the children of Israel from Egypt. It was to be a reminder that God had housed the people in tents and lived among them in a tent of His own, the "Tent of Meeting," which was a part of the portable tabernacle discussed in Week One, Day One. This feast, like others you'll find mentioned throughout the Bible, was observed on a specific day of the month every year. Look at the FEASTS OF ISRAEL chart on pages 40-41. Study the "Feast of Booths or Tabernacles" column and record in the margin of your Bible when this feast is observed annually.

Now read verse 1, verse 4, and verse 6 again, noting what month it is.

DAY FIVE

Today read chapter 3 again, this time marking distinctively every reference to *the people*. (Maybe you could use a symbol of a "stick man" like this: **people**.) In your notebook, list everything you learn about them on your list titled THE PEOPLE OF THE LAND. Make certain you include their leaders.

DAY SIX

Read Ezra 3:10-13. The remnant that returned to rebuild the temple held a celebration service right after the foundation was completed. Read these verses again. In your notebook, make a list of what you learn about this celebration service under the title THE CELEBRATION SERVICE. As you make your list, be sure to note the two different responses to the completion of the foundation. Why two responses?

Having completed your study of chapter 3, record the main theme of this chapter on your EZRA AT A GLANCE chart.

DAY SEVEN

Store in your heart: Ezra 3:11a: "They sang, praising and giving thanks to the LORD, saying, 'For He is good, for His lovingkindness is upon Israel forever.'" Read and discuss: Ezra 3:1-13.

QUESTIONS FOR DISCUSSION OR INDIVIDUAL STUDY

∾ Where was the house of God, the temple, to be rebuilt?

∾ Among the children of God, was anyone exempt from returning and participating in the rebuilding of the temple? Did everyone return to Jerusalem to help with the rebuilding project? Why do you think some did not return?

∾ According to what you learned this week in 1:1 and 1:5, what does God do if He wants you to do something? Has He stirred up your spirit to do something? Have you done it?

∾ Is giving to the work of God a biblical principle? How much did each person give? Are you giving to the work of God? How much are you to give?

∾ Can a blessing from God cause some degree of hardship on you as you accept the additional responsibility that the blessing brings? From where would the strength come from to carry this additional responsibility?

∾ Who was appointed to oversee the work on the temple?

∾ Who were the two leaders of the exiles mentioned in Ezra 3? Which one was the spiritual leader? Which one would have been the governmental leader? Why do you say that?

∾ God commanded the children of Israel to observe certain feasts. In chapter 3 they observed the Feast of Booths. What does this show you about their attitude toward obeying the commands of God? What caused them to go into captivity in the first place? Do you see a change in their attitude from what it was before the captivity? Explain what you mean.

∾ Why were some of the people weeping with a loud voice and some shouting aloud for joy?

THOUGHT FOR THE WEEK

For 70 years the children of Israel, separated from their temple, had not celebrated the feasts. The consequences of their disobedience had lasted a generation. God had initiated their release. Finally, they were home. Can you imagine what it must have been like to finally see in the distance the Promised Land they once possessed! On the other hand, however, what a heartbreaking sight it must have been for the old-timers to stand on the ruins of Solomon's magnificent temple. Sin is so costly. It not only affects the individual, but it also affects the community where that individual lives.

The children of Israel had paid the price of their disobedience...separation. Separation from family, separation from friends, separation from their homes, separation from their homeland, and most importantly, separation from worshiping God. Sin has the same effect on believers today.

The Feasts of Israel

Slaves in Egypt	1st Month (Nisan) Festival of Passover *(Pesach)*				3rd Month (Sivan) Festival of Pentecost *(Shavuot)*
	Passover	**Unleavened Bread**	**First Fruits**		**Pentecost or Feast of Weeks**
	Kill lamb & put blood on doorpost Exodus 12:6, 7	*Purging of all leaven* (symbol of sin)	*Wave offering of sheaf* (promise of harvest to come)		*Wave offering of two loaves of leavened bread*
	1st month, 14th day Leviticus 23:5	1st month, 15th day for 7 days Leviticus 23:6-8 *(1st and 7th days are Sabbath)*	Day after Sabbath Leviticus 23:9-14 *(It is a Sabbath)*		50 days after first fruits Leviticus 23:15-21 *(It is a Sabbath)*
Whosoever commits sin is the slave to sin	**Christ our Passover has been sacrificed** 	**Clean out old leaven... just as you are in fact unleavened**	**Christ has been raised...the first fruits** 	**Going away so Comforter can come** Mount of Olives	**Promise of the Spirit, mystery of church: Jews-Gentiles in one body**
John 8:34	1 Corinthians 5:7	1 Corinthians 5:7, 8	1 Corinthians 15:20-23	John 16:7 Acts 1:9-12	Acts 2:1-47 1 Corinthians 12:13 Ephesians 2:11-22

Months: Nisan—*March, April* • **Sivan**—*May, June* • **Tishri**—*September, October*

	Feast of Trumpets	Day of Atonement	Feast of Booths or Tabernacles	
Interlude Between Festivals	*Trumpet blown — a holy convocation*	*Atonement shall be made to cleanse you* Leviticus 16:30	*Harvest celebration memorial of tabernacles in wilderness*	
	7th month, 1st day Leviticus 23:23-25 *(It is a Sabbath)*	7th month, 10th day Leviticus 23:26-32 *(It is a Sabbath)*	7th month, 15th day, for 7 days; 8th day, Holy Convocation Leviticus 23:33-44 *(The 1st and 8th days are Sabbaths)*	New heaven and new earth
	Regathering of Israel in preparation for final day of atonement Jeremiah 32:37-41	**Israel will repent and look to Messiah in one day** Zechariah 3:9,10; 12:10; 13:1; 14:9	**Families of the earth will come to Jerusalem to celebrate the Feast of Booths** Zechariah 14:16-19	God tabernacles with men Revelation 21:1-3
		Coming of Christ		
	Ezekiel 36:24	Ezekiel 36:25-27 Hebrews 9, 10 Romans 11:25-29	Ezekiel 36:28	

Israel had two harvests each year—spring and autumn

But then God moved all history to bring about the release of His people. They had paid their debt. God did not destroy them or reject them. When the time was right, He came for His own. He stirred the hearts of those who were needed to bring about His plan. Whatever it took, God brought it about. He'll do the same for you.

When the children of Israel arrived home, they had had a change of mind, a change of heart. The discipline of God had brought about some good changes in their lives. Even though they were terrified of the people of the land, they still obeyed God by observing their feasts, by presenting their offerings, and by celebrating their dedication services openly, publicly. They were committed to trusting Him for whatever protection they needed. They had no army. Earlier, the enemy was used as an instrument of chastisement in the hands of a holy God; but now, this time, the hand of God kept their enemies at a distance.

He is an awesome God. He will do for us above all we can ever ask or think. We must simply trust Him and obey Him, doing what He tells us to do. He indeed is the Great Redeemer! We cannot escape Him, even in captivity!

OVERCOMING FEAR, DISCOURAGEMENT, AND FRUSTRATION

Where does fear come from? Why do the people of God have to deal with discouragement just like those who don't have a relationship with God? Why do those who serve God with the purest dedication and devotion face frustrations almost daily and at every turn?

The enemy's philosophy is, "If you can't join 'em, beat 'em!" If you would like to know what the enemy does in his attempt to keep you from doing what God has commanded you to do...then continue this study.

DAY ONE

This week you'll study chapters 4 and 5. Begin today by reading through chapter 4, marking *house* (also *temple*) in the same way you did in the previous chapters. Don't forget to add what you learn about the house of God to your list in your notebook.

Read Ezra 4:4-7. Make a list of the four kings mentioned in these verses. Underline the names of these kings in the text.

DAY TWO

Today your first assignment will be to read Ezra 4:1-5. As you do, mark in a distinctive way *the enemies of Judah and Benjamin*[4] (also called *the people of the land*[5]). You may want to use a black pen and draw a cloud like this  around each reference. Remember also to mark in the same way any pronouns that refer to them. Don't forget to ask the 5 W's and an H questions about these people. Again, add what you learn about them to your THE PEOPLE OF THE LAND list that you began last week.

Now go back and read Ezra 3:3 to learn how the Israelites reacted to the people of the land. Add this insight to your list.

Out of verses 4 and 5, what three things did the people of the land do to the children of Israel? (These three things may already be on your list—if not, add them.)

According to verses 5, 6, and 7, how long did this intimidation last (through the reign of how many kings)?

DAY THREE

Now there is something very, very important you need to be sure to see in the text of Ezra 4. If you scan Ezra 4, you will see that *house* (or *temple*) is marked in verses 1-5 and then again in verse 24, but is not mentioned at all in verses 6-23. This is because Ezra 4:6-23 is a parenthesis which interrupts the chronological order of this chapter. In other words, the chronological order of Ezra 4 is verses 1-5, then verse 24. Ezra 4:6-23 happened years after verses 1-5 and verse 24. In your Bible you may want to draw some straight lines down the margins on each side of these verses, such as ||. This will make these verses easy to spot and also will help you remember that this is a parenthesis and that there's a time change here.

Leaving out the parenthesis of Ezra 4:6-23, read 4:1-5, then verse 24. As you read, keep in mind that the main teaching in these verses is about the house of God. You'll deal with the parenthesis, Ezra 4:6-23, tomorrow.

Most scholars believe that Cyrus, the king of Persia, conquered the Babylonian Empire in the fall of 539 B.C. The exiles came back to Israel in 538 B.C. Now according to Jewish reckoning, the first year of their coming would have concluded sometime in 537 B.C., and the second year of their coming would have been sometime in 536 B.C. Last week you learned from your study of chapter 3 that, according to verse 8, the work on the temple began "in the second year of their coming to the house of God at Jerusalem in the second month," which would have been 536 B.C.

Now according to verse 4:24, what two significant events happened regarding the temple? Make sure these truths are on your HOUSE OF GOD list. If not, add them. According to 4:1-5, what caused the work to cease? According to THE TIMES OF EZRA, NEHEMIAH, AND ESTHER chart on page 46 what year did the work on the temple (the house of God) cease? Add this date to your "house" list, and write the year in the margin next to Ezra 4:24. You should have three dates now regarding the temple construction: one when the work began, one when the work ceased, and one for when the work resumed.

Read 4:4-7 again and see if you can understand why Ezra included this parenthesis in this chapter. Keep in mind the context and flow of thought through these verses.

THE TIMES OF EZRA, NEHEMIAH, AND ESTHER

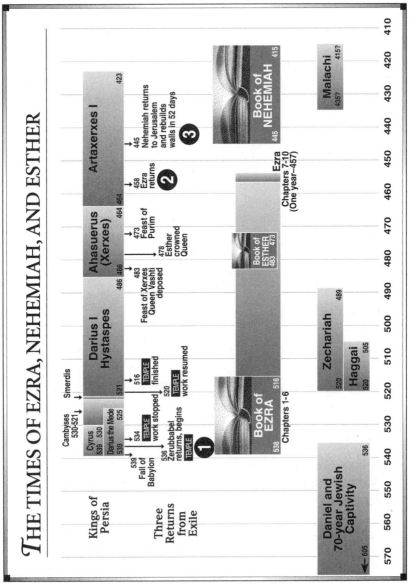

Was Ezra trying to point out how long the intimidating tactics of fear, discouragement, and frustration continued for *the people of the land* against the people of God—throughout the reign of Cyrus...throughout the reign of Darius...throughout the reign of Ahasuerus...and throughout the reign of Artaxerxes? If so, this would explain why Ezra inserted this parenthesis here. He wanted to show what *the people of the land* were doing to discourage, frighten, and frustrate the children of Israel.

DAY FOUR

Now read the parenthetical portion of Ezra 4:6-23. As you do, mark the words *city* and *wall,* each in its own distinctive way. Is it obvious now? Ezra is talking about the *city* and the *wall* in these verses and was talking about the *temple* in verses 1-5 and 24. Also, the TIMES OF EZRA, NEHEMIAH, AND ESTHER chart that you looked at yesterday helps you see that this is a parenthesis in time. The two kings Ahasuerus (Xerxes) and Artaxerxes reigned *after* the work on the temple began, ceased, and resumed.

Now in your notebook, under the headings THE SECOND LETTER OF EZRA (4:11-16) and THE THIRD LETTER OF EZRA (4:17-22), briefly list the main points of each of these documents. Ask the 5 W's and an H questions as you make these lists. Be sure to include answers to the following questions:

- According to this letter to King Artaxerxes, what were the children of Israel rebuilding?

- Is there any reference to the rebuilding of the temple in these verses?

Now that you have a better understanding of what verses 6-23 are about, what work do you think was stopped by force of arms—work on the temple or work on the city and the city walls?

Review chapter 4 and summarize the main message by recording your chapter theme on the appropriate line of the EZRA AT A GLANCE chart on page 66.

DAY FIVE

Your first assignment today is to read Ezra 5:1-5 and mark *house* the same way you have in previous chapters. Also include the marking of the synonyms *temple, structure,*[6] and *building*. Add what you learn to your HOUSE OF GOD list in your notebook.

Read these verses again, this time marking *decree* in a distinctive manner.

Now go again to the TIMES OF EZRA, NEHEMIAH, AND ESTHER chart on page 46. Find the two prophets Haggai and Zechariah on the chart and observe the dates they prophesied. Also locate Darius, the king of Persia, and note the dates of his reign. According to 4:24, the work on the temple began again *in the second year of Darius, the king of Persia*. If you haven't done so already, record the year in the margin of your Bible next to Ezra 4:24. How long had no work on the temple been done?

Read 5:1-5 again, answering these questions:

   a. Who was the governor of the province beyond the river?

   b. What question did he ask the children of Israel?

   c. Did the work on the temple stop?

   d. Why not?

DAY SIX

Read 5:16,17, marking *house, temple,* or *structure,* and *decree* the same way as before. Add to your lists anything new that you learn.

Again, there are seven letters or written documents contained in the book of Ezra. Other than the first one, all were written in Aramaic, the international language of those times. The first letter (1:2-4), written by Cyrus, was in Hebrew. You have seen and studied the first three of these letters or documents in 1:2-4; 4:11-16; and 4:17-22. The last four are found in 5:6-17; 6:2-5,6-12; and 7:12-26. Remember, because of the parenthetical portion found in chapter 4, these letters are not in chronological order. However, you can still study them as you come to them chapter by chapter. Just keep that in mind.

Read 5:6-17, "The Fourth Letter of Ezra," again asking the 5 W's and an H questions such as these: Who wrote this letter? To whom was it written? What question did Tattenai ask the Israelites? What was their response? etc. Make a list of the things you learn from asking these questions.

As you conclude your study of chapter 5, be sure to record your chapter theme on the EZRA AT A GLANCE chart on page 66.

DAY SEVEN

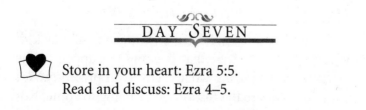

Store in your heart: Ezra 5:5.
Read and discuss: Ezra 4–5.

QUESTIONS FOR DISCUSSION OR INDIVIDUAL STUDY

∾ What did you learn from chapter 4 about the schedule of the work on the house of God? Have you ever started something that God told you to do and then stopped for whatever reason? Have you resumed that work yet? If not, what should you do?

∾ How did Ezra refer to the people of the land? Why did he refer to them in that way? What were they trying to stop the children of Israel from doing? What can you expect if you start to do the work of God?

∾ What did the people of the land try to do to the children of Israel? How did the children of Israel respond to this intimidation? How long did this intimidation go on? How long will the enemies of God try to intimidate you if you are doing the work of God?

∾ What prophets did God use to provoke the people of the exiles to resume the work on the temple again? Is God using this course to prompt you to resume something He told you to do in the past?

∾ What did you learn in chapter 5 about the eye of God toward the children of Israel? Why was God favorably disposed toward the Jews at this time? How does God look upon you today? Why?

THOUGHT FOR THE WEEK

Fear can often come from not knowing—the lack of knowledge. Not knowing what is going to happen in the future days. Not knowing what is going on presently. Not knowing from where the resources are going to come. Not knowing the results of the medical examination...the CAT scan…the MRI…the blood test…the biopsy. Uncertainties can dominate and rule a person's life.

Do we have to have all the answers? Must we have all the whys answered before we can move out with God? Is stepping forward without all the answers "blind faith"? No. Faith is not trusting in your understanding of the circumstances. Faith is trusting in His Word—believing that if God told you to do it, it will come to pass, and He will provide whatever you need to make that happen.

Surely the enemies of God will use fear, discouragement, and frustration to wear down those who are following God in obedience. We, like the exiles, must keep our focus on the task God has assigned us and resist the temptation of adopting the world's system into our labors just for the sake of convenience. Sometimes the offers are very attractive. When we decline those tempting morsels, rest assured that it won't be the end of it. Whatever the enemy can do to stop the work of God, he will spare no expense. He will freeze you into immobility with fear of the future. With discouraging events he can cause you to lose heart and have no desire to carry on. And he will send among you those who will deceitfully counsel you with bad advice that will result in failure after failure until your level of frustration reaches its peak.

The important thing is not to understand your circumstances. The important thing is to understand God and what He has instructed you to do. The enemy will come; that's a certainty. The question is, Will you continue to go on as directed by God? If you do, you can rest assured that the eye of our God will be on you, and your enemies will not stop you from doing His work.

GOD, WHERE ARE YOU?

What would you do if your most feared enemy walked up to you and cheerfully met a financial need in your life?

What would you do if a well-known unbeliever enthusiastically encouraged you to continue in your work with the Lord?

Does God use our enemies and the unbelievers in our lives to supply our needs and help us accomplish His work? Let's see what the Bible says about that!

DAY ONE

Today begin by reading 6:1-12, which contains the fifth and sixth letters. As you read these verses, mark *house* or *temple* (*its* when referring to the temple[7]) and *decree*[8] (*scroll*,[9] *edict*,[10] and *it* when referring to the scroll), adding to your lists in your notebook.

Verses 1-5 contain the fifth letter, and verses 6-12 contain the sixth. First read the fifth letter (verses 1-5), asking the 5 W's and an H questions. Record what you learn in your notebook under the title THE FIFTH LETTER OF EZRA.

Now read verses 6-12, interrogating the text. Record what you learn in your notebook under the title THE SIXTH LETTER OF EZRA. Make certain that you record what Tattenai was ordered to do, what he was ordered to provide, and what the penalty would be for those who did not follow these orders. Why did Darius order this done? In other words, what did Darius want the children of Israel to do for him?

DAY TWO

Read Ezra 6:13-22 and mark *house* or *temple,* and *decree.*[11] Add what you learn to your lists. Be sure to discover when the temple was finished. Now, according to the TIMES OF EZRA, NEHEMIAH, AND ESTHER chart, what year would that have been? Record the year in your HOUSE OF GOD list and in the margin of your Bible next to Ezra 6:15.

Make a list of the events that follow the completion of the temple. Pay particular attention to the feasts that were celebrated and when they occurred (if the dates are given). If you need to, refer to the FEASTS OF ISRAEL chart on pages 40-41 to find these dates.

Be sure to note what you learn about the priests and the people who participated in the Passover feast. How were they described? Also, who caused them to rejoice? What else had God done for them?

Now review chapter 6 and, in a summary statement, record the main theme of this chapter on the EZRA AT A GLANCE chart on page 66.

DAY THREE

For the remainder of your study of the book of Ezra, you will be working in what is referred to as the "second

segment" of the book. Ezra is divided into two main segments: chapters 1–6 and chapters 7–10. There is a lapse of
time of about 60 years between chapter 6 (the end of the first
segment) and chapter 7 (the beginning of the second segment). The events recorded in the book of Esther occurred
between these two segments of Ezra, during this 60-year
period of time. Most scholars believe that Ezra wrote this
book somewhere around 450 B.C. Therefore, the actual
writing of the events in the first segment of the book of Ezra
was done almost 100 years after they had actually occurred.

Today begin your study of this second segment by
reading chapter 7. As you read this chapter, mark *Ezra* in a
distinctive way. Notice that this is the first time you've seen
his name appear in this book. Remember to mark all the
pronouns that refer to Ezra *(he, him, his, you, your)*. Also
mark the first-person pronouns *I, my,* and *me,* which are
found at the end of the chapter. Because of the use of this
first-person pronoun, you can now see why Ezra is given
credit for the authorship of this book. As you mark *Ezra,*
make a list of what you learn about him. Make sure that
you pay attention to Ezra's genealogy. What priest was Ezra
a descendant of?

DAY FOUR

Read chapter 7 again, marking the following key words
and phrases in the same distinctive ways as you did before:

> *house of God*[12]
> *commandments (law)*
> *decree*[13]
> *the hand of God was upon him*
> any *time* phrases

Now with the time phrases in mind, look at THE TIMES OF EZRA, NEHEMIAH, AND ESTHER chart located on page 46 and discover the year Ezra "went up to Jerusalem" (verse 7). According to Ezra 7:6-10, when did Ezra and the sons of Israel leave Babylon? What day, month, and year would that have been? When did they arrive in Jerusalem? What day, month, and year would that have been? How long did the journey take?

Using THE TIMES OF EZRA, NEHEMIAH, AND ESTHER chart, compare Ezra's arrival in Jerusalem with the time of Zerubbabel's arrival. Note who was reigning as king during each of their times of ministry. Now you can clearly see the lapse of time between the two segments of Ezra.

DAY FIVE

Read Ezra 7:11-26. This is the seventh and final letter or decree found in the book of Ezra. Make a brief list of the main points of this letter in your notebook under the title THE SEVENTH LETTER OF EZRA. Record the main theme of chapter 7 on the EZRA AT A GLANCE chart on page 66.

DAY SIX

Read chapter 8, marking all the key words and references to time as you've done in the previous chapters. Add any new insights to the appropriate lists.

Now fill in the chart on Ezra on the next page.

This chart will help you organize the truths you learn about the events in the life of Ezra as he brings the exiles back to Jerusalem. After you complete the first event, go to the next ones in consecutive order.

Summarize chapter 8 by expressing the main theme of this chapter in a brief statement and recording it on the EZRA AT A GLANCE chart. Add other insights as appropriate.

Ezra, Leader of the Exiles		
The Scripture	What Ezra Did	The Results of His Actions
(8:15-20)		
(8:21-23)		
(8:24-30)		
(8:31-34)		
(8:35,36)		
(9:1-4)		
(9:5–10:4)		
(10:5-44)		

DAY SEVEN

 Store in your heart: Ezra 8:22b.
Read and discuss: Ezra 6:6-22; 7:27,28; 8:21-23.

QUESTIONS FOR DISCUSSION OR INDIVIDUAL STUDY

∾ According to Ezra 5:2, what did the children of Israel begin to do? (Keep this in mind as you answer the next few questions.)

꙳ What did King Darius tell Tattenai to do? What did King Darius tell Tattenai to provide? How was Tattenai to do this? What would be the penalty for anyone who would not follow King Darius' orders? What was the response of Tattenai and his colleagues to the king's orders?

꙳ Did God use a man who desired to see the work of God stopped to provide for His work? Could God use some of your enemies, those who would like to see your work for Him stopped, as vessels for your provision?

꙳ Does God provide whatever is needed to do whatever He instructs us to do? Is He providing for you? Are you doing what He has told you to do?

꙳ What day, month, and year was the temple completed? How long was the temple under construction? Why did it take that long? Could it have been completed sooner? What halted the construction? When they were released from captivity, what were the exiles to return and do? Did they continuously do what they had been set free to do?

꙳ What did the exiles do after the temple was completed? What feasts did the exiles observe shortly after the completion of the temple? When were these feasts to be observed? Why do you think they observed these feasts?

꙳ How is Ezra described? How would someone describe you? What was his heart set on? What is your heart set on?

꙳ Why do you think the hand of God was upon Ezra? Is it evident that the hand of God is upon you?

∾ What did Ezra do after all the people were assembled at the river? Why? What was his request of God? What did God do? Do you ask God for all your needs? Did God answer his prayer? Does God answer your prayers?

THOUGHT FOR THE WEEK

Have you ever thought of your enemies as part of God's provision for you? Have you ever considered the nonbelievers who are in positions of authority as sources of encouragement to you to do the work of God?

As we studied through these chapters, it is amazing to see how God took the very people that the children of Israel would normally avoid and used them to meet their needs. Maybe we need to change our perspectives about our enemies and unbelievers! Could they, in fact, be a blessing and not the curse we always see them as?

God was evident in Ezra's life. Everyone noticed the difference—the believers and the nonbelievers. What made the difference in Ezra's life? Did he do anything special that caused God to favor him? If so, what was it, and can you do it? Ezra had set his heart to do three things: to study the Word of God, to practice it, and to teach it. If I set my heart on these same three things, would the hand of God be upon me? Would people be able to see the hand of God upon my life?

HOW MUCH DOES SIN COST?

Someone once said that sin will take you further than you ever intended to go, keep you longer than you ever intended to stay, and cost you more than you ever intended to pay. We can see that illustrated in the book of Ezra.

DAY ONE

Read chapter 9 and mark *Ezra* (and any pronouns that refer to him, such as *I*, *my*, *me*) and any reference to the *house of God*. As you read chapter 9, mark in a distinctive manner any other repeated words that you may see as being key to this chapter.

Now add what you learn about Ezra from verses 1-4 to the chart EZRA, LEADER OF THE EXILES in the "What Ezra Did" column (page 57). These should be brief statements of what he did in reaction to the news he had just been given.

DAY TWO

Read chapter 9 again today. As you do, make a list of what you learn about the people of Israel. Ask the who, what, where, when, why, and how questions as you read the text—questions such as: What had they done? What was a name that was used to describe them (verses 8,13,15)? Why did Ezra use that term to describe them? This questioning process will cause you to slow down your reading so that you can discover all the facts about the people. Remember, these things were written for our instruction (Romans 15:4). As always, record what you learn in your notebook.

DAY THREE

If you didn't mark the word *commandments*[14] (*commanded*[15]) in Day One, read through chapter 9 and do so now. In your own words, what commandment had the people broken?

Read Exodus 34:10-17 and look for the answers to the following questions:

> ∾ What did God command them not to do?

> ∾ Why did He command them not to do that?

> ∾ What would be the result of not keeping this commandment?

DAY FOUR

Read Deuteronomy 7:1-11 and look for answers to the following questions:

> ∾ What did God command them not to do? Why?

> ∾ What did God say about the children of Israel?

∿ What did God say about those who hate Him?

∿ How does this relate to what they had done in Ezra 9?

DAY FIVE

In Ezra 9:5-15 we have Ezra's prayer after he received the bad news about the sin of the people. On the EZRA, LEADER OF THE EXILES chart, fill in the first column, "What Ezra Did," adjacent to 9:5–10:4.

Review what you learned from chapter 9 and record the main theme on the EZRA AT A GLANCE chart on page 66.

Now read chapter 10:1-4. Mark *Ezra* and the pronouns.

DAY SIX

Read chapter 10:5-44 and mark any references to *house of God, commandment,*[16] and any time phrases as you have done before. Record them in the appropriate places.

Make a list in your notebook of the main points of the proclamation that was sent out to all the people of Israel. As you do, note when certain events occurred, according to the text.

According to verse 44, who else was "put away" besides the foreign wives?

Summarize the main teaching or subject of chapter 10 and record this summary statement on the EZRA AT A GLANCE chart. Also review all the chapter themes of Ezra, and record the main theme for the entire book in the appropriate place on the EZRA AT A GLANCE chart.

(Hint: This would be a summation of what the themes for Ezra 1–10 are about.) Add any additional insights required to complete the chart.

DAY SEVEN

 Store in your heart: Ezra 9:6-8.

Read and discuss: Exodus 34:10-17; Deuteronomy 7:1-11; Ezra 9:5-15; 10:1-17.

QUESTIONS FOR DISCUSSION OR INDIVIDUAL STUDY

- What sin did the people of Israel commit?

- Who was involved in this sin?

- What was Ezra's response when he heard about this sin?

- What was the response of those who "tremble at the words of the God of Israel"?

- According to verses 5-15, what did Ezra do?

- What did you learn about Ezra's prayer? What were the main points of his prayer?

- Why did Ezra say that God had shown them "a brief moment of grace"? What did God want them to do?

- According to 9:7, what will God do if His people sin?

- What happened while Ezra was praying?

- What was the people's confession?

- What was their solution to rectifying this sin?

- What proclamation was made?

~ What was the penalty for not obeying the stipulations of the proclamation?

~ What did Ezra tell them to do when they gathered in Jerusalem?

~ What proposal did the people offer in order to accomplish this act of repentance?

~ Was the proposal accepted? Opposed? By whom?

~ Who was affected by the sin of intermarrying?

THOUGHT FOR THE WEEK

No one acts alone. Everything we do affects someone else. Sin has a devastating effect. It contaminates all it touches, all that it comes into contact with. Because of the intermarrying of the exiles with the people of the land, God's judgment *had* to come. The people had such a short memory...less than a hundred years had passed!

Only one generation, and the cycle was already being repeated. Had the fathers forgotten to teach their sons and daughters the Word of God? Is that why Ezra was dispatched by God—because of such a time as this? Ezra, a man of the Word of God, arrived on the scene of moral decay, and immediately the conviction of sin fell upon the people. No one summoned the people—they came. Weeping, they confessed their sin openly, repented, and put it away. Yes, it was costly. Yes, it was painful. But it was necessary.

God has sent and will continue to send His prophets, priests, and scribes to His people to declare His Word. It's the only solution for a crooked and perverse generation. Who will be the next Ezra? Might it be you?

EZRA AT A GLANCE

Theme of Ezra:

SEGMENT DIVISIONS

Author:	YEARS COVERED	CENTRAL CHARACTERS		CHAPTER THEMES
Date:				1
Purpose:				2
				3
Key Words:				4
				5
				6
				7
				8
				9
				10

Nehemiah

OVERCOMING FEAR AND DISCOURAGEMENT

∾∾∾∾

They had just returned from Jerusalem and Hanani was anxious to see his brother, Nehemiah. As they visited, Nehemiah asked about Jerusalem and the Jews still living in the land. "They are not doing well, Nehemiah." He described a people distressed and embarrassed. Why? Hadn't the temple been rebuilt 60 years earlier? Hadn't the people been allowed to return to their land, the Promised Land? Ezra had been back in Jerusalem for 13 years. What could be wrong?

"Nehemiah, the wall of Jerusalem is broken down and its gates are burned with fire." The truth gripped Nehemiah. He wept—he wept as he had never wept before. For days he could not compose himself; he just wept and prayed before the Lord.

Why? The walls had been torn down for 150 years. The news that they were still down would be no news at all. I believe Nehemiah wept because the mighty hand of a sovereign God gripped his heart, and the Spirit of God whispered in his ear, "Nehemiah, how long will My name suffer this insult? My temple has been rebuilt, but it stands naked in a city without walls. My people, called by My name, live in fear because the city where I am worshiped is unprotected. A city without walls, Nehemiah, is no city at all. Nehemiah, build My walls."

It was one of those moments in the life of a follower of God when God changes his perspective. Nehemiah's life would never be the same. His comfort zone was dissolving around him, and life was about to change radically. Have you been there?

With change often comes fear. With obedience often comes discouragement. We find ourselves challenged from within and from without. But Nehemiah overcame the fear and the discouragement. Do you want to live in fear and discouragement? No? Study Nehemiah with us. As we study this book together, we will see the principles he used, and how to apply them to our own lives.

KNOWING GOD
AND HIS PROMISES

How do you overcome fear and discouragement? This week we will learn what Nehemiah did when he faced these feelings.

DAY ONE

Ezra and Nehemiah were originally one book. Parts of each were written in first-person narrative, indicating they were written by Ezra and Nehemiah, respectively, and later compiled into book form by an editor. Many believe the editor was Ezra himself.

If you studied Ezra, you are familiar with the historical setting of Ezra. Nehemiah was his contemporary, coming to Jerusalem just 13 years later. Today, refamiliarize yourself with the historical setting by reading chapters 1 and 2 of Nehemiah. You may also want to read pages 23-26 of the Ezra study to remind yourself of the context.

DAY TWO

Read Nehemiah chapter 1 again, paying close attention to the prayer recorded in verses 5-11. Nehemiah records

71

several prayers in his book. As we study Nehemiah together, find a distinctive way to mark each prayer that Nehemiah records. I suggest something like an asterisk (*) in the margin next to the first verse of each prayer. This will make it easy to locate each prayer in the book. You will also find it helpful to keep a record of what you learn about praying as we work our way through this book. Only mark verses 5-11 today. We will get to the other prayers later in our study.

From time to time I will ask you to mark certain key words in your Bible. You will find it helpful to keep a record of the words you have marked and a list of what you learn by marking those words. Read pages 9-11 for a suggestion on how to do this.

Today as you read chapter 1, mark every reference to *God.* You will need to mark this word throughout Nehemiah. Keep a list of everything you learn about God while studying Nehemiah. Also, mark the words *remember* and *command*[1] *(commanded, commandments*[2]) in distinctive ways. Record what you learn in your notebook.

Does chapter 1, verse 8 sound familiar? He is quoting Leviticus 26:33—a passage we looked up while studying Ezra. It all fits together, doesn't it?

DAY THREE

As we have seen in Ezra, it is often helpful to read other passages in the Bible that relate in some way to the one you are studying. This is called cross-referencing. Today let's cross-reference Nehemiah's prayer with the prayer of another Jewish exile, Daniel. Daniel and Nehemiah were not contemporaries. Daniel's vision had been recorded many years earlier. Read Daniel's prayer recorded in Daniel 9:1-19. Then reread Nehemiah 1:5-11 and record the similarities between the two prayers in your notebook.

DAY FOUR

The similarities between Daniel's prayer and Nehemiah's are amazing, aren't they? Although they were recorded and prayed years apart, they reflect the same heart attitude. Do they reflect your heart attitude when you pray for your country?

Today read Daniel 9:20-24. In the first year of Darius, the son of Ahasuerus (538 or 539 B.C.), the angel Gabriel appears to Daniel to give him understanding concerning the first coming of the promised Messiah. Gabriel's time reference in verse 24 is usually translated "weeks." The Hebrew word literally means "sevens." It can be used to indicate seven days, weeks, months, or years. In verse 24, we are told that 70 weeks or, literally, 70 sevens have been decreed. That would be 490. Since the events foretold did not occur within 490 days, weeks, or months, it is logical to assume that the 70 "sevens" refers to years. When does the countdown start? After you read Daniel 9:20-24, compare it with Nehemiah 2 to find the answer.

DAY FIVE

The decree to rebuild Jerusalem was issued by Artaxerxes in the year 445 B.C., and Nehemiah was sent to do the work. As you studied in Ezra, the decree to rebuild the temple was issued by Cyrus. The decree described in Daniel was to rebuild the city, not just the temple. Gabriel had told Daniel 93 years earlier that the decree would be issued and Jerusalem would be rebuilt. God writes history in advance!

Today read Nehemiah 1:1–2:8, noting every reference to time, such as is found in 1:1 "…in the month of Chislev…." Mark time references with a clock in the margin, as we showed you on page 9 in the "How to Get Started" section. These time references help establish the flow of the history and enable us to interpret the story in its historical context. When you have finished, record the main event(s) of Nehemiah 1 on the AT A GLANCE chart located on page 106. Don't be intimidated by this chart. It is for your use, and yours alone. No one is going to grade you on your answers. Just write down a statement that describes what happened in this chapter so you can remember Nehemiah—at a glance.

DAY SIX

Read Nehemiah 2. You will be introduced to two new characters who will play an important part in this story. They are Tobiah and Sanballat—the enemies, the bad guys. Sanballat was the governor of Samaria; Tobiah was one of his officials. Mark their names in a distinctive way as you read chapter 2, then mark them every time they are mentioned in Nehemiah. You could simply underline them. The phrase, the *hand of my God* is a key phrase in both Ezra and Nehemiah. Mark this or similar phrases in Nehemiah 2, then go back to Ezra 7 and 8 to review what you have already learned about "the hand of God." In a distinctive way, mark each reference to *sad(ness)*.[3] Later we will mark each reference to *joy*. You may want to mark both of these words with the same color and put a / through *sad* or its synonyms. For example: s&d.

Record the main event(s) of Nehemiah 2 on your AT A GLANCE chart.

DAY SEVEN

 Store in your heart: Nehemiah 1:8,9.
Read and discuss: Nehemiah 1,2.

QUESTIONS FOR DISCUSSION OR INDIVIDUAL STUDY

- ∾ What did you learn about God as you studied Nehemiah 1 and 2? How is God described?

- ∾ What did you learn specifically about "the hand of God"? From Ezra and Nehemiah?

- ∾ How will this newfound knowledge of *the hand of God* help you overcome fear and discouragement?

- ∾ What did you learn about prayer this week? How specific were the requests? How specific were the confessions of sin? How specific are yours? On what basis were the appeals to God made? In other words, what did Daniel and Nehemiah believe about God that enabled them to seek His face and ask His forgiveness?

- ∾ What have you learned about praying for your country?

THOUGHT FOR THE WEEK

One of the keys to overcoming fear and discouragement is to know the Word of God. God is sovereign, and what He says will come to pass. In 538 or 539 B.C. God told

Daniel that Jerusalem would be rebuilt. He also gave Daniel a countdown for the events leading up to and surrounding the crucifixion of our Lord. In 445 B.C. Nehemiah approached the king of Persia and was given permission to rebuild the city of the Lord. The countdown to Messiah being "cut off" or crucified, began.

Once again we see God writing history in advance. While there is no direct indication that Nehemiah was familiar with the prophecy of Daniel, we do know that Daniel was very well-known by the exiles and was famous in Persia. Another prophet of Israel, Ezekiel, mentioned him in such a way as to indicate his reputation was well-known (Ezekiel 14:12-20). So, Nehemiah probably knew the writings of Daniel. Do you see the courage we would gain if we knew what God had said and believed that He meant it?

People who know their God have the courage not only to face people, but also the courage to face Him. You saw as you studied the prayers this week that both Daniel and Nehemiah approached God on the basis of His mercy. Have you grasped that truth? He is a merciful God. He can be approached even when you have failed. Approach Him, admit your failures, confess your sins, and ask for forgiveness. You will find His mercy. Daniel and Nehemiah approached God based on the belief that He is a promise-keeping God. They reminded Him of His promises (not that He had forgotten them) and asked Him to do what He said He would do. As you study the Word of God, you will become familiar with the promises of God and be able to claim them in prayer as these two men of God did. That's a good reason to study, isn't it!

In chapter 2, verse 2, we have the first mention of fear. We see that Artaxerxes asked Nehemiah why he looked sad—Nehemiah was "very much afraid." In spite of his fear, Nehemiah presented his request. Where did he get the courage? His strength came from his prayer in chapter 1. From this, we learn that the size of our courage depends on the depth of our prayer life. To have courage you must believe God. To believe God, you must know God. To know God, you must study His Word. Do you know God? The only other option is to live in fear and discouragement.

ARMING YOURSELF WITH THE SWORD OF THE SPIRIT

ᴼᴼᴼᴼ

This week we will see the strategy of the enemy and the response of Nehemiah. The truth will set you free.

DAY ONE

Nehemiah 3 is an overview of the building program. Nehemiah explains who was responsible for what repairs. Read chapter 3 and mark each geographical reference, such as "the Sheep Gate." Since there are so many locations, it would be best to simply underline each reference with a colored pencil or marker. In your notebook, under the heading WHO BUILT THE WALL, list the occupations of the workers who participated in the project. Watch for the mention of any carpenters or masons.

In this chapter we have the first mention of Eliashib, the high priest. This is probably the same man mentioned in Ezra 10:6. Highlight or underline his name with a colored pen or pencil. It will be important to see his relationship to Sanballat and Tobiah later in the story.

When you have finished, record the theme of Nehemiah 3 on your AT A GLANCE chart.

Jerusalem's Gates in Nehemiah's Time

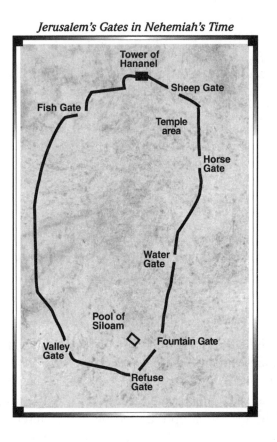

DAY TWO

Chapters 4–6 describe some of the problems faced by Nehemiah and others as they repaired the walls of Jerusalem. Today, read Nehemiah 4. Mark each reference to *wall* and *work*.[4] As you read, you will notice another prayer of Nehemiah. Mark it in your Bible just as you did the prayer in chapter 1. Also mark the references to *Sanballat* and *Tobiah* just as you did in chapter 2.

DAY THREE

Opposition to the work of the Lord is not new, and neither are the enemies' tactics. The method of the enemy of God—Satan, the devil—is never new or original. He uses the same tactics today that he used in 445 B.C. As we read today, I want you to look for the tactic the enemy used in his attempt to stop the work of the people of God in the city of Jerusalem. Read chapter 4:1-6. Notice the method that Sanballat and the others used to try to stop the work. The key is in verse 1.

Fear and Discouragement		
The Enemy	Tactics of the Enemy	Response of the People of God
	Fear—2:2	Prayer—1:5-11; 2:4

On a page in your notebook start a three-column chart like the one above. Use this chart to learn how to overcome fear and discouragement by seeing the enemy's tactics and the response of Nehemiah and the people of God. After you finish reading, record what you learn from 4:1 on your tactic chart. Also, from 4:6, record the reason the people were able to build the whole wall to half its height despite the harassment of Sanballat. In other words, what was the mind-set of the people that enabled them to overcome this tactic of the enemy? Also take note of any direct response the people made to Sanballat and his friends. Did the people answer Sanballat back?

Before you start today's assignment, record on your FEAR AND DISCOURAGEMENT chart what you learned from Week One.

DAY FOUR

During your study yesterday, did you see the tactic the enemy used in Nehemiah 4? He mocked them (4:1). How did the people overcome the mocking and jeering of the enemy? They had made up their mind to do the work of God, or as the NIV says, "they worked with all their heart" (4:6). They ignored the mockers and continued in the work.

Today read Nehemiah 4:7-23. Mark each use of the word *God* or any words that refer to Him, such as LORD. Add what you learn about God to the list in your notebook. As you read, I want you to consider whether or not the people responded in faith. Were they trusting God?

We will discuss this idea more later.

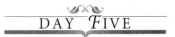

DAY FIVE

Read Nehemiah 4:7-23 again. Watch for the tactic the enemy uses in this section of chapter 4. Pay close attention to the way Nehemiah overcomes this tactic. Mark the key words *fear, afraid,* and *remember.* Add what you learn about these key words to your notebook. After you have done this, add what you learn about the tactics of the enemy and the response of the people to your FEAR AND DISCOURAGEMENT chart. When you finish, record the theme of Nehemiah 4 on your AT A GLANCE chart.

DAY SIX

Some of the assignments this week have been long, and I thank you for being diligent to do the work. The church today desperately needs men and women who are willing to search out the Scriptures and see what God has said.

You have a good handle on Nehemiah 4. Today I want you to read it one more time slowly, out loud. As you read, watch for the military strategy the Jews were using. Were they wrong to have an aggressive military posture? If they trusted in God, should they have been armed and on guard? Is it wrong for a Christian police officer to be armed? Is it wrong for a Christian to be in the military? Think about it.

DAY SEVEN

 Store in your heart: Nehemiah 4:14,20.
Read and discuss: Nehemiah 3–4.

QUESTIONS FOR DISCUSSION OR INDIVIDUAL STUDY

- ∾ What occupations were represented by the people building the wall? Were there any carpenters? Masons?

- ∾ What does this teach us about "wall-building" in the church today? Who can build the wall in the church today?

- ∾ What tactic was first used to discourage the workers in chapter 4? How did the people respond to this tactic? Next time the enemy comes against you in this way, how will you respond?

∽ What was the enemy's second tactic?

∽ How did the word *remember* help you understand how to respond to this second tactic of the enemy?

∽ Discuss what it must have been like to have been a co-laborer with God, rebuilding the walls. Have you been in the center of God's will, yet facing opposition? How did you respond?

∽ Is fear wrong? Were the Jews or Nehemiah wrong to fear? Did they act on their fear? How?

∽ What about the issue of armed guards? Were they right or wrong? Were they still walking in faith or in fear?

THOUGHT FOR THE WEEK

In Ezekiel 13, God speaks against the false prophets because they did not rebuild or repair the wall around the house of Israel. He doesn't mean a physical wall. The wall God has in mind is far more important than anything made of rocks and mortar. The wall is our understanding of the Word of God. The Word surrounds us and protects us. It is the Word that keeps the enemy from penetrating the recesses of our soul. It is the Word that secures us in times of uncertainty. It is the Word that provides a peace that passes understanding. It is the Word that secures our joy. The Word increases our faith.

How is your wall? Are there holes in it? Each day that you do your homework, you are adding one more brick to your wall. The enemy will attack. Satan will do everything possible to distract you from your mission. He will do everything possible to destroy your time. He hates strong-walled Christians because "the people who know their God will display strength and take action" (Daniel 11:32b).

They are a threat to his plans. Follow Nehemiah's example. First, "remember the LORD who is great and awesome," and second, "fight for your brothers." As you do this study, find prayer warriors who will watch in prayer while you build in the Word, then you watch over them in prayer while they build.

Did you notice how many carpenters and masons were listed as workers in rebuilding the wall? Not one. The wall was not built by professional wall builders. It was built by regular, ordinary folks. You cannot leave the wall building in your life to professionals. You are responsible to build the wall yourself. God gives us the responsibility to obey and the freedom to act. We have been invited to be co-laborers with Christ.

Nehemiah and the people trusted the Lord. They armed themselves and worked. They were even willing to be co-laborers in battle, if need be. Did they lack faith? No. They were ready for whatever God chose to do. Are you ready? Are you ready to give a defense of the faith that is within you? As you do this study, you are building your wall, and at the same time, you are arming yourself by becoming familiar with the Word of God, the sword of the Spirit.

KNOWING THE TACTICS
OF THE ENEMY

The tactics of the enemy, Satan himself, have changed little over the years. Knowing what he does and what I have in Christ will help me to be an overcomer.

DAY ONE

Read Nehemiah 5:1-13. There is a shift in focus here from the building of the wall to another problem. The story moves from conflict from without, to conflict from within. Pay close attention to the sins the people have committed. As you read, mark every reference to *God* and add what you learn about Him to your list in your notebook. Also mark every reference to *fear* and add any insights you glean to your chart on fear in your notebook. Then cross-reference this passage with Leviticus 25:35-37.

DAY TWO

Yesterday you saw the sins of the wealthy. Nehemiah was wealthy. Today we will see his example to the elite of Judah. The governor under the Persian system had the right to tax the people for his salary and expenses. But the people were already overburdened. Read Nehemiah 5:14-19. As you read, pay close attention to Nehemiah's example and continue to mark *God, fear,*[5] and the other key words. What does Nehemiah do? Why does he do it? We have another prayer in this passage, so be sure to mark it. Don't forget to record the main event(s) of Nehemiah 5 on your AT A GLANCE chart.

DAY THREE

Sanballat and the boys are at it again. Mocking did not stop the work on the wall. Neither did the threat of physical violence. But the enemy has other tactics to cause fear and discouragement. In chapter 6 we see some of those tactics being used, and we see how wall builders render those tactics useless.

Read Nehemiah 6:1-9. Add to your FEAR AND DISCOURAGEMENT chart the two tactics you see in this passage and how the man of God responds to them. Watch for Nehemiah's prayer. Also mark the word *wall* as you did in Nehemiah 4.

DAY FOUR

Today let's read Nehemiah 6:10-19. What are the tactics the enemy uses in this passage? Add them to your chart, along with the responses of Nehemiah.

Be sure to mark each of Nehemiah's prayers in this chapter. Also mark the words *frighten*[6] and *wall.*

DAY FIVE

Nehemiah 6:10-19 can be a little hard to follow. Let's spend today looking at it one more time to be sure we are following the flow of thought.

Shemaiah was one of the priests, and for whatever reason he was shut up at home. When Nehemiah came to visit him, Shemaiah said that Nehemiah's life was in danger. The solution Shemaiah presented to Nehemiah was for them to hide themselves within the temple. As a layman, Nehemiah was not allowed in the temple.

Read Nehemiah 6:10-19 slowly, out loud. Do you see why Nehemiah reacted the way he did? Watch for the response of the prophets and prophetesses to Nehemiah. By the way, this Noadiah is not the same as the one you saw mentioned in Ezra 8:33. The one here is a prophetess who is only mentioned here. Write the theme of Nehemiah on your AT A GLANCE chart.

DAY SIX

How am I to overcome the fear and discouragement of the enemy? How did Nehemiah? How did the people of God? One way was by knowing the truth. Knowing the truth kept Nehemiah from believing Shemaiah and Noadiah, and therefore he overcame the plot of the enemy. Let's look at some other passages that, if we apply the principles in them, will help us to overcome instead of being overcome.

First read 2 Timothy 1:7-10. What have we been given? Second, read John 14:27. The question is the same: What have we been given? The last passage I want you to consider is more lengthy, but it is worth your time because the lesson learned here will set you free. Read 1 Samuel 17:41-50. To whom does the battle belong?

DAY SEVEN

 Store in your heart: Nehemiah 6:9.
Read and discuss: Nehemiah 5–6; Leviticus 25:35; 1 Samuel 17:41-50; 2 Timothy 1:7-10; John 14:27.

QUESTIONS FOR DISCUSSION OR INDIVIDUAL STUDY

∽ What was the problem Nehemiah had to deal with in chapter 5? In the Leviticus 25 cross-reference, what is the point concerning charging interest? Jesus said the law could be summed up in two commands: Love the Lord your God with all your heart and love your neighbor as yourself. How does Leviticus 25:35 fit with this command? How we treat others is extremely important to God. How do you treat those around you who are in need?

∽ How did Nehemiah correct the problem? Do you lead by example? What are ways we tell our children to love each other and then fail to lead by example? How does the enemy try to discourage and distract in chapter 6?

∽ Has an enemy ever used threats of blackmail, true or not, to try to stop you from the work of the Lord? What were the specific instances? How did you react?

∽ What lessons do we learn from Nehemiah's reaction to the insult? How should we react? How did Nehemiah react to threats of physical violence? Is God able to protect me, even against physical violence? What if He allows me to be hurt or injured?

- ∽ How was Nehemiah able to discern that Shemaiah and Noadiah did not speak for God? In other words, where does this kind of discernment come from? Are you learning to discern?

- ∽ Discuss what you learned when you cross-referenced 2 Timothy 1:7-10 and John 14:27.

- ∽ How can understanding 1 Samuel 17:41-50 help you walk in courage?

THOUGHT FOR THE WEEK

On the surface, there was nothing wrong with the request from Sanballat and Geshem. They made it sound as though they simply wanted a meeting to discuss the work that was being done. But Nehemiah would not be distracted from the Lord's business. There really was nothing to discuss. He was about the Lord's business, and they were intent on stopping him. There was no reason to pause in the work, rest in the accomplishments, or negotiate with the enemy. He, like the people of 4:6, had a mind or, more literally, a heart, to work. Is your heart, your mind-set, to do the work of the Lord? Are you firm in your conviction? If you waver, the enemy will gain a foothold. Had Nehemiah wavered, the enemies of the Lord would have killed him.

The second tactic, the lies and threats of blackmail, is still used to distract us from the work of the Lord. Do you find yourself frightened by such tactics? Respond as Nehemiah did: Tell the truth, and stay at the work to which God has called you. Blackmail is one of the most common tactics of the enemy. Telling the truth disarms the devil. One of the more subtle tactics used by Sanballat is found in 6:5. The fifth time Sanballat sent a letter, he did not seal it. This was a grievous insult to the position and rank of Nehemiah, as the custom of the day demanded the letter be wrapped in fine cloth and sealed. How do you handle insults? How do you react when you are treated without respect? How did Nehemiah react? Apparently he took no notice of the insult. How should we respond? Remember what your mother told you when you were young? That's right. Just ignore them. Nehemiah did.

REMEMBERING THE GOODNESS OF GOD

This week we will see revival break forth as the people of God hear the Word of God and remember the goodness of God.

DAY ONE

The wall is built. The enemy is frustrated. The men and women of God refused to believe the lie that God was not powerful enough to protect them. The enemy shouted and threatened, but it was to no avail because the old, roaring lion was toothless (1 Peter 5:8,9). If God is for us, who can be against us?

Today you will study Nehemiah 7. This is essentially the same list you read in Ezra 2. There are some discrepancies between the two lists (which are hard to explain). The totals of the two lists are the same—42,360 (Ezra 2:64; Nehemiah 7:66). In Ezra we have 29,818 people listed. In Nehemiah we find 31,089 people listed. In Ezra we find 494 people mentioned who are not mentioned in Nehemiah. In Nehemiah we find 1765 people who are not found in Ezra. If we add the surplus of people found in Nehemiah (1765) to the list in Ezra (29,818), we find a total of 31,583. By adding the surplus of people found in Ezra (494) to the number of people found in Nehemiah (31,089), we have a total of 31,583. The two lists seem to correct each other. When we subtract 31,583 from the total given in both Ezra and Nehemiah, 42,360, we find 10,777 people not listed. The 10,777 not named may have been excluded by name for several reasons. It is possible that the 10,777 could not prove their family registry, as some of the Levites had been unable to do (Ezra 2:62,63; Nehemiah 7:64,65). Or it is also possible they were not of the tribe of Judah or Benjamin, and therefore were not named.

Whatever the explanation, we know that in the mind of Ezra and Nehemiah there was no contradiction. As you know, the two books were originally one. For the lists to have both been included in one book, the editor must have understood them as being noncontradictory. The Word of God does not contradict itself, and God made no mistakes when He inspired the men who wrote it.

Today read Nehemiah 7. Underline the various groups of exiles who are returning, just as you did when you studied Ezra 2. Notice how carefully the list is laid out. What you are reading is a list of people who were saying to God, "Yes, Lord, I want to be a part of rebuilding the temple." As the body of Christ, we also have responsibilities and privileges in the service of our God.

Don't forget to write the theme of Nehemiah 7 on your AT A GLANCE chart.

DAY TWO

I know yesterday was a little difficult, but ferreting out the truth is always worth the trouble. Hang in there!

The book of Nehemiah divides at 7:73b. Up to this point the focus has been on the work of rebuilding the walls of Jerusalem, and the work was successful. The walls were rebuilt. This division is called a segment division. I am sure that you have noticed on your AT A GLANCE chart the vertical columns to the left of the chapter numbers. This is where you can record the segment "The Work."

Now the focus of the book changes. No, I am not going to tell you the new focus—you have to read and discover it on your own. Read chapter 8:1-8 and mark every reference to *law* (don't forget any pronouns referring to it). We marked *commandment* on Day Two of our first week together, so I suggest that you mark *law* the same way. Also mark *worshiped* in a different, distinctive way.

DAY THREE

Read Nehemiah 8:9-18. This time, in addition to *law*, look for and mark every reference to *joy* along with its synonyms, such as *rejoicing*,[7] or antonyms, such as *mourn*. Mark them the same way you did on Day Six of Week One. In chapter 8, expressions of time are very important, so you will want to mark those as well. When you have finished, don't forget your AT A GLANCE chart.

It would be helpful to cross-reference this passage with Leviticus 23:34-44.

DAY FOUR

In chapter 8, Ezra reads the law to the people, and the Levites explain the meaning of the passages to the assembly. You see the response of the people as they are confronted with the Word of God. They celebrated the Feast of Booths or Tabernacles, and they held a solemn assembly. Today you will begin a study of that solemn assembly.

Do you remember from our study in Ezra the purpose of the Feast of Booths or Tabernacles? If not, go back and read page 36 (Week Two, Day Four) in this book to refresh your memory.

Read Nehemiah 9:1-15. As you read, mark every reference to *God* and *worshiped*.[8] Be sure to add what you learn about these to your list.

DAY FIVE

Today read Nehemiah 9:16-31, again marking every reference to *God* just as you did yesterday. Add what you are learning about Him to your list. By now your list on God is impressive. When you have finished today's assignment, take time to worship Him by reading over the list you have on God and meditating on the truths you have learned.

DAY SIX

You have done a lot of work this week, but it has been time well-spent. Today you will finish your study of Nehemiah 9. There is so much more to learn from this passage, but we must move on. In the future, if you have time, it would be interesting to mark every reference to *the sons*[9] (or *descendants*[10]) *of Israel* (usually *they* or *them*) in chapter 9, and list what you learn about them and their attitude toward God. For now, read 9:32-38 and mark every reference to *God* and *commandments*[11] *(law)*. Add what you learn to the lists in your notebook. Don't forget your AT A GLANCE chart.

DAY SEVEN

 Store in your heart: Nehemiah 9:6.
Read and discuss: Nehemiah 7–9.

QUESTIONS FOR DISCUSSION OR INDIVIDUAL STUDY

∾ In chapter 8, Ezra read the law to the people, and the Levites gave the understanding. What was the initial response of the people? Look for the words *grieved* and *mourn*. Why did they respond that way? How do you respond to the Word of God?

∾ Discuss the similarities between the sins of Israel and the sins of America. What about you personally? From what you learned in chapters 8 and 9, how are we different from the Israelites in our response to God? Or are we?

∾ From your study this week, what did you learn about the purpose of the solemn assembly? How could you apply the truths concerning a solemn assembly to your own life?

∾ What did you learn about God this week?

∾ Remembering what God has done in your life is very powerful and encouraging. For a month, you might want to try keeping a journal of what God is doing in you personally. At the end of the month, read it and rejoice over what you see that the Lord has done.

THOUGHT FOR THE WEEK

In Nehemiah 8, history occurs right before our eyes. Men, women, and children gathered to hear the reading of the law. Ezra climbed the great platform and laid the scroll upon the podium. As he began to open the scroll, the people stood in one accord. Ezra blessed the Lord, the great God. The people raised their hands toward heaven and shouted, "Amen! Amen!" With their hands lifted, they affirmed Ezra's worship of the great God and made Him their own. Then, bowing down, they worshiped the Lord with their faces to the ground. That was only the beginning! As Ezra read the Word of God and the Levites gave the understanding, the people began to weep over their sin. Real revival! This is not the kind of revival we talk about today—we use the word too loosely. Revival usually describes a special series of meetings at the local church. This week you read about a real revival. The Word of God was read and explained, the people of God were convicted of their sin, repentance broke loose, worship entered—and revival came!

God sends revival. It comes as His Holy Spirit brings us to a realization of where we are and where we should be. There are some things you can do to make yourself open for revival. You can take your worship seriously, just as they did. You can expose yourself to the Word of God so it has opportunity to challenge you, just as they did. You can confess your sins and commit before God to walk in righteousness, just as they did.

Are you ready for revival? Are you open to revival? If God sends revival, will your heart be tender to His prompting?

SEEING WHAT GOD HAS DONE

DAY ONE

As you studied last week, you saw a people confronted by the Word of God and convicted of their sin. Today read Nehemiah 10 and watch for the result of revival: the commitment of the people. Chapter 9 closes with an agreement, in writing, between the people and God. The first 28 verses of Nehemiah 10 list the names of the men who signed the covenant. The rest of the chapter is...oh, you read it. Marking the word *we* will help you see what is going on. Be sure to keep marking *God* and *law (commandments)*.[12] If you have time, list in your notebook everything the people are promising. Record on your AT A GLANCE chart the theme of chapter 10.

DAY TWO

Remember when we studied Nehemiah 7? You read that the city was large and spacious, but the people were few, and the houses were not built. Today we will see how the leaders handled this problem.

Today read Nehemiah 11. As you read, watch for major groups such as *the sons of Judah*[13] or *sons of Benjamin*,[14] who are involved in the action. Underline these major groups. Also take notice of the percentage of the people who are chosen. When you have finished, record...oh, you know what to do, don't you.

DAY THREE

Nehemiah 12 is an exciting chapter! The walls have been built, the enemy has been overcome, and the law has been read. What happens next? We will study Nehemiah 12 to find out. Today I want you to read verses 1-30 of this chapter. While you are reading, again underline every reference to the *Levites (sons of Levi)*, as you did in chapter 11. The story line begins near the end of your reading assignment. Follow the story carefully, and pay close attention to the word *purified*.

DAY FOUR

Nehemiah 12 is a celebration! The priests, the people, and the singers have gathered to dedicate the wall. They started by purifying the priests, the Levites, the people, the wall, and the gates. The purification process was symbolic of dedicating themselves to God. They were giving the walls, the gates, and themselves to God. Seems like a proper first step to celebration, doesn't it? As you saw yesterday, the Levites, the singers, and probably many of the people, were summoned to Jerusalem to see what God had done.

In the rest of Nehemiah 12, we will see how God's wall was put on display.

Today read chapter 12:31-47. As you read, follow the route taken by the two choirs on the map on page 80. Consider two questions as you read today:

1. How much of the city did they walk around?

2. How loud were they?

Don't forget to mark *God, law (command),*[15] and *worship.*[16] Then record the main event of Nehemiah 12 on your AT A GLANCE chart.

(If you have ever been to Jerusalem, this passage will come alive! I can picture the walls of the old city and imagine the celebration. We at Precept Ministries take a tour group to Israel each year. Come with us sometime. Your Bible study will never be the same!)

DAY FIVE

Our last days together in this study will be in chapter 13 of Nehemiah. Nehemiah stays in Jerusalem for 12 years before returning to the court of Artaxerxes for a period of time. Chapter 13 details incidents which occur while he is gone and his response to them when he returns. Today read Nehemiah 13:1-9. Pay close attention to who is excluded from the assembly of God. Mark the name *Tobiah* (and any pronouns) just as you did earlier in our study. When you finish, read Nehemiah 2:10 to refresh your memory concerning Tobiah. Also, mark *law* and *God* as you have been doing throughout this study. Then add any new insights to your lists.

DAY SIX

Today finish reading Nehemiah 13. As you read, watch for three specific problems addressed by Nehemiah. We have seen Eliashib the high priest mentioned several times during our study. Today, watch for his name as you read. To whom is he related by marriage?

The final problem addressed in this text is one Ezra also had to deal with. When you have finished reading, cross-reference Nehemiah 13:23-29 with Ezra 9 and 10. Look at how each man handled the same problem.

When you finish, fill in your NEHEMIAH AT A GLANCE chart for chapter 13. Also fill in the last segment division for chapters 8–13.

DAY SEVEN

 Store in your heart: Nehemiah 12:43,44.
Read and discuss: Nehemiah 10–13.

QUESTIONS FOR DISCUSSION OR INDIVIDUAL STUDY

∾ In chapter 10, what exactly were the people promising to do?

∾ How would those commitments apply to us as New Testament believers?

∾ How was the wall of Jerusalem dedicated? What was the significance of walking on top of the wall, completely around the city? Could the celebration have been heard by those who had attempted to stop the work on the wall? Why is that significant?

∾ What did you learn by marking the word *joy* and its synonyms?

∾ According to chapter 13, who was to be excluded from the assembly? Why?

∾ What did you learn about Tobiah?

∾ Intermarriage, tithing, keeping the Sabbath—why were these such big issues? Should we be concerned about them today? What are the principles the church today needs to apply?

∾ How did Nehemiah deal with the problems? How had Ezra dealt with them almost 30 years earlier? What can we learn from these two styles?

∾ How did the people move from revival back into the same old sin patterns? Discuss ways the church today does the same thing. What is the answer?

THOUGHT FOR THE WEEK

The word went out, "Come to Jerusalem." They came. The Levites, the singers, the band—they all came to Jerusalem. Can you imagine the excitement they must have felt when they saw the wall? For many this was probably their first time to see the wall that God had built in Jerusalem. When the choir was assembled, Nehemiah gave a personal tour. Half of the assembly went to the left and half to the right, and they marched up the steps to the top of the wall. Then they walked the length of Jerusalem, on top of the wall—the wall the enemy had tried to stop. The wall Tobiah referred to when he mocked the Jews saying, "If a fox should jump on it, he would break their stone wall down" (Nehemiah 4:3). The wall that struck fear in the heart of the enemies because they knew God was behind the building of it (Nehemiah 6:16). As they walked on their tour, can't you hear them singing praises to God because of what He had done? When the people gathered at the temple to worship, the noise was so loud that the mockers could probably hear them worshiping. What an awesome God! He built a wall in 52 days using unskilled labor. He built a wall so strong that the multitude could walk on top of it. No wonder they worshiped!

But what happened next? In Nehemiah 10, 11, and 12, we have revival, rejoicing, and worship. In chapter 13, we have the same old sin pattern that got them into trouble before. Apathy happened. It is an insidious sin that comes in slowly, quietly, without notice. We slip into it. Only a little at first, but then more and more as we become distracted by the cares of the world. It happened in the days of Nehemiah, and it happens today. We see one answer to apathy in Nehemiah 13. The answer is accountability. While Nehemiah was there, they were faithful. We need someone in our life to hold us accountable.

Are you accountable to another believer? Is there someone in your life who can and will "call you on the carpet" concerning your walk with the Lord? If the answer is no, then you are in as much danger as the people of Israel. Start with the people at your church. Find a small group of like-minded believers and be accountable to them. It is one way to prevent the apathy that has the potential to destroy us.

Another way is to stay accountable to the Word of God. Constantly exposing yourself to the truth of God by studying His Word will stop the drift toward old sin habits. The Word will keep you on course. As you study, you will be transformed by the renewing of your mind. God's Word promises that (Romans 12:1,2).

Can you believe you have worked your way through Nehemiah in only five weeks? It has been an awesome study. During the first three weeks, we looked at overcoming fear and discouragement. Now you know some of the tools the enemy uses, and you have seen the example of Nehemiah and Israel in overcoming. Keep overcoming— you are more than a conqueror through Jesus Christ our Lord.

The last two weeks we looked at real revival and the apathy that so often comes on the heels of revival. Watch yourself. Take heed lest you fall. May the Lord keep you thirsty for the Living Water and hungry for the Bread of Life as you continue in the study of Esther.

Nehemiah at a Glance

Theme of Nehemiah:

SEGMENT DIVISIONS

Author:			CHAPTER THEMES
Date:			1
			2
Purpose:			3
			4
Key Words:			5
			6
			7
			8
			9
			10
			11
			12
			13

ESTHER

In Such a Time As This

❧❧❧❧

Life and events can often seem very ordinary, even insignificant. Yet you never know what God is doing behind the curtains of time nor where it will lead. That is why it is so important that we live godly in the everyday circumstances of life, as you will see in your study of Esther.

LIVING GODLY IN THE EVERYDAY CIRCUMSTANCES OF LIFE

"For such a time as this." You may have heard the phrase quoted before, but I wonder if you realize how significant it is for your own life, for the days in which *you* are living: The times are critical—critical for the welfare of our nation and crucial to your future if you are a child of God. That's why the study of the book of Esther is such a significant and timely one. Although the title of this book of the Bible is the name of a woman, there is a man in this true-life story who is every bit as much the hero as the heroine for which it was named. There's much to learn from the characters of this strategic real-life drama—much that we need to know and live by, so study well, Beloved. The results could become a launching pad to propel you into a destiny you never dreamed you could or would attain.

DAY ONE

Read Esther 1. As you do, mark every reference to time with a clock so that you can establish the historical context of the book. Also mark the words *angry*[1] *(anger, wrath*[2]*)* and *edict*[3] in a distinctive way. When you finish, do the following:

1. Record in your notebook the main characters mentioned in this first chapter, along with a brief description of what you learn about each of them. You could put this in a chart like the one at the bottom of this page. Examine the text to see what you observe when you ask the 5 W's and an H: who, what, when, where, why, and how.

2. Look at the references to time that you marked and then consult the chart THE TIMES OF EZRA, NEHEMIAH, AND ESTHER on page 46. Note how the book of Esther relates chronologically with Ezra and Nehemiah.

3. Look at the map on page 113 to see the geographical territory that the Persian Empire encompassed. History tells us that King Ahasuerus' (Xerxes') predecessor, Darius I, had invaded Greece and was defeated in 490 B.C. Esther chapter 1 occurs seven years later in 483 B.C. It was during the time of Ahasuerus' banquet, in the third year of his reign, that a council was called to plan another invasion of Greece.

The Main Characters in the Book of Esther				
King Ahasuerus	Queen Vashti	Esther	Mordecai	Haman
Reigned from India to Ethiopia over 127 provinces				
Capital was Susa				

PERSIAN EMPIRE
in relationship to other nations

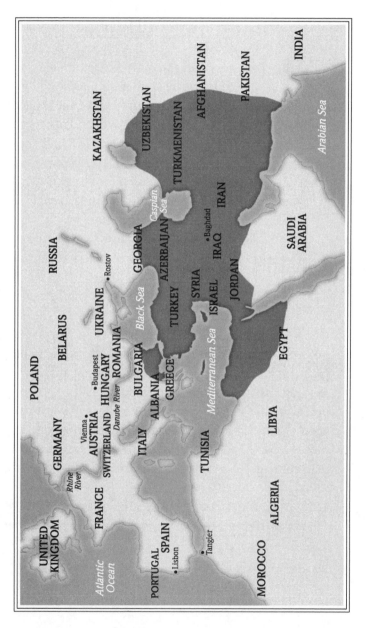

DAY TWO

Esther is a great and fascinating drama taken from the pages of biblical history. Read chapter 2 and watch as some significant new characters are introduced into this drama.

Mark the word *Jew* in a distinctive way. You might want to draw two triangles to make a star of David like this ✡. Coloring it blue would help you spot its occurrence rather easily. As you mark the word, also mark any synonyms or pronouns in the same way (for example, *people* in verse 10). Also mark every reference to time.

When you finish the chapter, note when Esther is taken to King Ahasuerus. How many years have elapsed since chapter 1?

According to history, the four-year gap between chapters 1 and 2 correlates with the period of the Persians' Greek campaign. King Ahasuerus (also known as King Xerxes) assembled probably the largest military force ever seen, including a large navy. He made a mistake by not sending his troops by sea. Instead he had his men build a bridge at the Hellespont (a one-mile-wide strait between the Aegean Sea and the Sea of Marmara, which separates Asia Minor and Thrace in modern-day Turkey). See the map on page 113. It was this delay which gave Sparta time to assemble 30 city-states to help resist the Persians. The army of Ahasuerus barely defeated Sparta at the Battle of Thermopylae and then moved to Athens, where they ravaged and burned part of the city. However, they were then lured to the sea, where they were defeated at Salamis. King Ahasuerus watched the destruction of his navy from a high mountain, went home to Susa defeated, and chose his queen.

DAY THREE

Read through Esther chapter 2 again today and record what you learn about Esther and Mordecai on the chart in your notebook entitled THE MAIN CHARACTERS IN THE BOOK OF ESTHER. When you finish, consider what you observed about Esther as a person and about Mordecai and his character, especially as seen in the event surrounding the king. God tells us in Romans 15:4 and in 1 Corinthians 10:11 that the things which were written in earlier times were written for our encouragement, our instruction, and our perseverance. When we study the lives of others who lived for the Lord, it gives us courage. When our lives become difficult, we will not be tempted to quit or give up, but to persevere as we observe how God comes to the aid of those who really trust Him.

DAY FOUR

As you read through the third chapter of Esther today, you will meet another character who plays a significant role in the events that follow.

From this point on, mark *Haman, the son of Hamme-datha the Agagite* in a significant color or way; however, do not mark every reference to Haman—only those which identify him as an Agagite. Also mark the following key words and their synonyms: *Jew, edict*[4] *(decree, decreed*[5]*), destroy,* and any reference to time.

As you mark the references to time, note the timing of these events in comparison to chapter 2. Also note when

Pur, the lot, is cast before Haman, when the edict against the Jews is written, and when the edict will be executed.

According to Babylonian tradition, the gods met the first month of the year to decide men's fate—thus, the possible timing of the casting of Pur.

DAY FIVE

Read through chapter 3 again today and think about the significance of the events which transpire in this chapter. Record on your chart all that you learn about Haman. Also record any new insights you observe about King Ahasuerus and Mordecai. Carefully read Esther 3:3,4 and note Mordecai's reason for not bowing to Haman.

Now record the main events covered in chapters 1–3 under the chapter themes on the ESTHER AT A GLANCE chart on page 133. Instructions on how to do this are in the "How to Get Started" section on page 11.

Haman offered the king 10,000 talents of silver—a sizable sum in light of the king's defeat in Greece and the loss not only of many men and ships, but also of the booty of war. Herodotus, a historian, wrote that the total annual revenue of the Persian Empire was 14,560 talents. When Alexander the Great conquered the Persians, his booty at Susa was 49,000 talents.

DAY SIX

As you read chapter 3, did you wonder why Mordecai, who seemed loyal to King Ahasuerus, refused to bow down to Haman as the king commanded? When you marked the phrase *Haman, the son of Hammedatha the Agagite*, it became obvious that the author of Esther wanted the readers to understand exactly who Haman was—so much so that he uses the phrase two times in just ten verses.

While 2 Samuel 14:4; 18:28; and 1 Kings 1:16 show it was customary for Jews to show respect by bowing to their kings, in the Persian culture when one bowed to his king, it was done as an act of worship to one he considered a divine being. Yet, there may have been another reason that Mordecai refused to bow.

If you have a *New Inductive Study Bible,* you will see an insight box in the margin of Esther 3 which tells you that the term *Agagite* could possibly be a synonym for an Amalekite. Agag was king of the Amalekites. If Haman was an Amalekite, it would give us another possible explanation as to why Mordecai would defy the king's command and refuse to bow down to Haman.

Read Exodus 17:8-16 and 1 Samuel 15:1-35. In your notebook record what you learn about the Amalekites and their relationship to the Jews from these two passages. Remember, Mordecai's reason for not bowing to Haman was the fact that he, Mordecai, was a Jew.

DAY SEVEN

Store in your heart: Esther 1:17.
Read and discuss: Esther 1:17; 2:5-15; 3:1-15.

QUESTIONS FOR DISCUSSION OR INDIVIDUAL STUDY

∾ To store something in our hearts means to memorize it, and although Esther 1:17 does not seem like a verse one would choose to remember, what principle can you learn from it in respect to the influence of those in positions of authority? Are there any lessons for life that you can apply practically to your own life in any way? Discuss them.

∾ Who are the main characters in the first three chapters of Esther?

a. Discuss what you learned about the character of each. If you are short on discussion time, focus your discussion on Esther and what her behavior in chapter 2 tells you about her character.

b. Have you seen anything about the characters in these first three chapters that is applicable to today? What did you learn about Esther that would help you discern the character of others or yourself?

∾ What did you learn about the Agagites or Amalekites that would explain Mordecai's reason for refusing to bow to Haman?

a. What did you learn about the Amalekites from Exodus 17? The Amalekites fought Israel, but according to this passage who else would have war against them from generation to generation? Do you think Mordecai could have been familiar with Exodus? Why?

b. What did you learn about Agag and the Amalekites? What does Samuel's action with respect to Agag show you about him and Agag?

c. Did you pick up any practical insights from 1 Samuel that you can apply in your own life? Maybe a new understanding of God and how He views partial obedience to very specific commands?

Thought for the Week

We live in a time, an era, when Christendom is very focused on self, on the individual—on what God can do for us and how Christianity benefits us. We look for what is expedient for us, rather than for what is biblically right and in keeping with the reality that God is God and we exist through Him and for Him—not for ourselves. There is a lack of submissiveness about our walk. We seek our own individual rights, privileges, and plans.

The book of Esther gives us another glimpse of life—a life in which the world doesn't center around us and fit into our scheme, our order of events, our preferences. We would do well to gaze long and hard at these historical scenes and contemplate them in light of the way we live and how we could live.

Queen Vashti was dethroned, so to speak, because her apparently blatant disregard of her husband's command set an improper example for the women of the land. Esther may have had other plans, other dreams and aspirations, but she submitted herself to the headship of her cousin. That act of obedience—difficult though it may have been, combined with her willingness to admit that she didn't know it all and, therefore, needed wise counsel—would earn Esther a throne...and more!

And then there's the issue of loyalty! Would Mordecai's loyalty to his king remain unrewarded? Did it matter? Or did it matter only to Mordecai that he did what was right? As we look at Mordecai in this opening act of a drama yet to be unfolded in time, we need to ask ourselves if we act to be seen and rewarded, or if we do what is right simply because it is right—and because there is a God in heaven to whom we will someday give an account.

Is there a God in heaven who looks down upon the hearts of men and women and rules and overrules hearts of kings and the edicts of man in favor of those who are His? It would be a good question for you to resolve in your thinking, and the book of Esther will help you. The book of Esther is not only a gripping drama—it can have a dramatic impact on your life and, consequently, impact the society in which you live. I pray it will provoke you to live godly in the ordinary circumstances of life, knowing that the ordinary is God's preparation for that moment when God pulls back the curtain and lets you see how He has moved through you in an extraordinary way.

WHEN ALL SEEMS DARK AND HOPELESS

When things seem dark and hopeless, do you wonder, "Is there a God in heaven who rules over the affairs of man? A God whom I can trust to be there in my deepest need, my hour of crisis? A God who is never too late?"

If you could have a positive answer to these questions, can you imagine the quiet confidence, the boldness that would be yours?

The lessons for the next two weeks should give you your answer. Study well, observe the Word of God, and discover truth for yourself: You will be all the richer, Beloved.

DAY ONE

Read through Esther 4 and mark the following key words in the same way you marked them last week: *Jews, destruction,*[6] and *edict (decree*[7]*)*. Take careful note of the events of this chapter.

DAY TWO

The edict sent to the provinces allowed the Jews only 11 months of survival. Their fate seemed sealed, for once a law was invoked, according to the laws of the Medes and

Persians, it could not be changed. The permanence of a Persian law made by the king is affirmed in Daniel 6:15. What recourse did these people have? How could God possibly rescue them?

Read chapter 4 again. This time mark the following key words in distinctive ways: *sackcloth, ashes,* and *fast(ing).* Add the word *fasting* to your key word list. Then note exactly who put on sackcloth and ashes and fasted and why they did so. Record your insights in your notebook. (From your study of Ezra and Nehemiah, you also saw that they fasted: Ezra 8:21; 10:6; Nehemiah 1:4.)

Read Esther 4:14. What do you think gave Mordecai the confidence that if Esther remained silent, then deliverance would arise from another place? Read Jeremiah 33:14-26 and list God's statements regarding the future of Israel in your notebook. (By the way, Jeremiah prophesied from 627–574 B.C. He was in Jerusalem during King Nebuchadnezzar's final siege and destruction of Jerusalem and the temple.)

DAY THREE

Although God is never mentioned by name in the book of Esther, which makes it unique among the other books of the Bible, it seems obvious from Mordecai's and the Jews' sackcloth, ashes, and fasting that they were looking to the God of heaven for deliverance.

Look up the following Scriptures, and record in your notebook what you learn about fasting. As you read these passages (which are not exhaustive), examine each in light of the 5 W's and an H and note what you learn from them in respect to sackcloth, ashes, and/or fasting. You may want to mark these three words in the following Bible passages the same way you did in the book of Esther.

∾ Joel 1:1-14 (Joel prophesied from 825–809 B.C.)

∾ Jonah 3:1-10 (Jonah prophesied from 784–772 B.C.)

∾ Isaiah 58:3-12 (Isaiah prophesied from 739–681 B.C.)

   *Note that Esther covered the years 483–473 B.C., thus the Jews would have knowledge of these prophets and historical events.

DAY FOUR

Read chapter 5. Mark key words and references to time. Then when you finish, note Esther's response to Mordecai in chapter 4 and her strategy in chapter 5. Also note on the chart that you began last week, THE MAIN CHARACTERS IN THE BOOK OF ESTHER, what you learn from chapters 4 and 5 about Esther and Mordecai.

DAY FIVE

Read Esther 6 and carefully observe the progress of events in this chapter. When you finish, note what you learn about King Ahasuerus and Haman in Esther 4–6. Record this on your chart entitled THE MAIN CHARACTERS IN THE BOOK OF ESTHER. Also record your chapter themes for chapters 4–6 on the ESTHER AT A GLANCE chart.

DAY SIX

Read through Esther 2:5–6:14 and watch the chain of events. Note all the references to time that you have marked as you studied. What do you observe in this chain of events? In the timing? Do the events seem accidental?

Look up the following Scriptures. Record in your notebook what you learn about God and the events of life from these passages:

    ∾ Deuteronomy 32:39

    ∾ Daniel 4:34,35

    ∾ Isaiah 43:13

Do you think the fasting of the Jews, Mordecai, and Esther played any role in these events? Do you think God had anything to do with it all—or are they mere coincidence? Think on these things. What can you learn for your own life?

As you bring this week to a close, take a few minutes to think through the content of Esther chapter by chapter. What is the main event covered in each chapter of Esther? Record that on the ESTHER AT A GLANCE chart on page 133. Then when you finish, see if you can think through Esther chapter by chapter all the way through chapter 6, without looking at the chart. When you do this, it helps you remember the Bible book by book, which really comes in handy when you are ministering to others and you want them to see what God says in respect to their particular situation.

DAY SEVEN

 Store in your heart: Esther 4:14.
Read and discuss: Esther 4–6.

QUESTIONS FOR DISCUSSION OR INDIVIDUAL STUDY

∾ Review the course of events in the book of Esther from chapters 1–6.

ᘗ The book of Esther can be an interesting and insightful character study. Discuss what you learned about the following people and what you can apply to your own life:

- King Ahasuerus
- Queen Vashti
- Mordecai
- Esther
- Haman

ᘗ What did you learn from the two passages on fasting? Discuss what you learned about fasting—the way it was done, how it was done, and why it was done.

ᘗ Finally, where do you see God in the events of Esther to this point—or do you think He is totally disassociated from these events since He is not mentioned?

THOUGHT FOR THE WEEK

When you are in trouble, where do you turn? Why? Where does *your* help...your hope...come from?

Is man really able to rescue man? Or is the unseen God behind the curtains of life's stage, overseeing the events of your life, the lives of others, the actions of nations?

Your answers to these questions can be the difference between peace or turmoil, between stability or emotional and mental chaos. Are you trusting God, seeking God, Beloved? If not, may we suggest that you consider why you are not?

> Thus says the LORD,
> "Cursed is the man who trusts in mankind
> And makes flesh his strength,
> And whose heart turns away from the LORD.

For he will be like a bush in the desert
And will not see when prosperity comes,
But will live in stony wastes in the wilderness,
A land of salt without inhabitant.
Blessed is the man who trusts in the LORD
And whose trust is the LORD.
For he will be like a tree planted by the water,
That extends its roots by a stream
And will not fear when the heat comes;
But its leaves will be green,
And it will not be anxious in a year of drought
Nor cease to yield fruit" (Jeremiah 17:5-8).

UNDER THE CRUSHING THUMB OF MAN OR HELD IN THE MIGHTY HAND OF GOD?

Are you frustrated by the plans, plots, and actions of other people? Do you feel controlled by others, a victim of their power?

Can God not override man? Or must He surrender His people, His plan, and His purposes for them to the devices of man?

Study well...the answers are in the Book of books—the Bible!

DAY ONE

Read through Esther 5–7 to put yourself back into the context of the book. As you do, mark any key words that you have marked in the other chapters. Then record the main event covered in chapter 7 on your ESTHER AT A GLANCE chart. When you finish, read Esther 8 and mark every occurrence of the word *revoke(d)*.[8] Although you have seen this before in your study, note what could not be revoked and why. (Remember Daniel 6:15.)

DAY TWO

Read Esther 8 again. This time mark key words and any reference to time. List in your notebook the details of the

127

new edict—written and sealed with the king's signet ring. When you finish, record the main event of this chapter on your AT A GLANCE chart.

DAY THREE

Read Esther 9–10 and mark key words and all references to time. Also mark the phrase *but they did not lay their hands on the plunder* (or similar wording). When you finish, review the events of this chapter in your mind and record the events covered in these final chapters on the AT A GLANCE chart. Then you will have a good summary of the book of Esther.

DAY FOUR

Reread Esther 9 and note that once again the king issues another edict. Record the details of this edict in your notebook. When you finish, go back through Esther and note every edict recorded in this book. You might want to give your list the heading THE EDICTS OF THE BOOK OF ESTHER. Also record these edicts under the segment divisions on the ESTHER AT A GLANCE chart and fill in as much of this chart as you can.

DAY FIVE

Read Esther 9 one more time and mark every reference to *Pur* and *Purim*. Then go back to 3:7 and mark *Pur* the same way. When you finish, record in your notebook all that you learn in respect to Purim. Answer as many of the

5 W's and an H as the text gives you in respect to this feast, noting what it is, why it was inaugurated, when it occurs, how it is celebrated, and why. Also make sure you note why it is called Purim. This is a feast still celebrated annually by the Jewish people.

DAY SIX

On your final day of study, note all you learn about the king, Haman, Esther, and Mordecai on the chart THE MAIN CHARACTERS IN THE BOOK OF ESTHER from chapters 7–10. Then reflect on all that you learned, especially about Mordecai.

Is Esther the only hero in this historical account? What do you learn from Mordecai's life that you can apply to your own life? What kind of a role model is he?

From all that you learned in your study these past three weeks, who do you think is behind Mordecai's promotion? Why? Do you think he could have spoken Esther's famous words, "If I perish, I perish"? And what about you? How committed are you to God and to the welfare of the people of His kingdom?

DAY SEVEN

    Store in your heart: Esther 10:3.
Read and discuss: Esther 7–10.

QUESTIONS FOR DISCUSSION OR INDIVIDUAL STUDY

∾ What is the sequence of events in Esther 7–10?

a. Discuss the various edicts recorded in the book of Esther.

b. What made an edict of the king so important?

c. Could the edict of the king ordering the destruction of the Jews on the thirteenth day of the twelfth month, Adar (see Esther 3), be revoked? What Scripture in Daniel tells of the strength of a Medo-Persian king's edict?

d. Did you see any significance in the fact that the Jews knew about the edict of chapter 3 eleven months before it was to be enacted?

e. How did the Jews survive this edict? Discuss what was put into place to counteract it, how and when it was executed, and the outcome of this edict.

∽ Did you learn anything in respect to these edicts that you could apply to your own life? Read the questions at the beginning of this week's assignments and tell how you would answer these questions after studying these past three weeks.

∽ What new insights did you record in respect to King Ahasuerus, Haman, Esther, and Mordecai?

a. Discuss how each of them fared and why.

b. How does Mordecai compare to Esther? Is she the only "hero" of this book?

c. Share what you learned from each of the lives of the main characters of this book that you can apply to your own life?

d. What insights did you get from their lives in respect to people and their behavior?

∞ How would you explain the feast of Purim to another person? Cover as many of the 5 W's and an H that you can in respect to this feast.

∞ Finally, share what touched you the most as you studied the book of Esther. Do you think it will have any lasting impact on your life? How? What are you going to do to make sure that you will not lose the principles and precepts you have discovered in this book?

THOUGHT FOR THE WEEK

"If I perish, I perish." These are words we associate with the person of Esther, a Jewess who lived almost two-and-a-half millenniums ago. But as children of God, should that not be true of us also? Were we not called by our Lord Jesus Christ to deny ourselves, take up our cross, and follow Him? Are we not to lose our life, "to perish," so that through our death His resurrection life might be manifested in the darkness of the time and, thus, impact our society—saving many lives through our unwavering, uncompromising witness?

Can you imagine, Beloved, what an impact such consecration, such denial of self, would have on a society that is so self-absorbed?

If only we would realize, as did Esther and Mordecai, that we have been brought to "His kingdom" for such a time as this and, consequently, live accordingly. Live—fearing neither the face nor the threats of man, but fearing only to disobey the heavenly edicts of God!

If we were to do this, our Christianity would take on a whole new dimension of power. Surely we would see and experience the supernatural deliverance of our sovereign, omnipotent God. And from the ranks of Christendom there would be more of whom it could be said, "They sought the good of God's people and spoke for the welfare of His kingdom." May it be said of you…of us.

ESTHER AT A GLANCE

Theme of Esther:

SEGMENT DIVISIONS

		CHAPTER THEMES	Author:
		1	Date:
		2	Purpose:
		3	Key Words:
		4	
		5	
		6	
		7	
		8	
		9	
		10	

NOTES

Ezra

1. NIV: also *you did not listen*
   KJV: *ye have not hearkened*

2. NIV: *temple*

3. NIV: also *temple*

4. KJV; NKJV: *the adversaries of Judah and Benjamin*

5. NIV: *the peoples around them*

6. KJV; NKJV: *wall*

7. KJV: does not use *its*

8. NIV: also *order, decreed*

9. KJV: *roll*

10. KJV: *word*

11. NIV: also *command*
    KJV; NKJV: *commandment*

12. NIV: also *temple*

13. NIV: also *letter, order*
    KJV; NKJV: also *letter*

14. NIV: *commands*

15. NIV: *gave*

16. NIV: *commands*

Nehemiah

1. NIV: *gave, commands*
   KJV: *commandedst*

2. NIV: *commands*

3. KJV; NKJV: *sorrow*

4. NIV: also *worked*
   NKJV: also *construction*

5. NIV: *reverence*

6. NIV: also *intimidate*
   KJV: *afraid, fear*
   NKJV: also *afraid*

7. KJV; NKJV: *gladness*

8. NIV: *worshiping*

9. NIV: *the Israelites*
   KJV; NKJV: *the children of Israel*

10. NIV: *of Israelite descent*
    KJV: *of Israelite lineage*
    NKJV: *the seed of Israel*

11. NIV: *commands*

12. NIV: *commands*

13. NIV: *the descendants of Judah, people of Judah*
    KJV; NKJV: *the children of Judah*

14. NIV: *descendants of Benjamin, people, the descendants of the Benjamites*
    KJV: NKJV: also *children of Benjamin*

15. NIV: *commands*
    KJV: *commandment*

16. NIV: *service*
    KJV: *word*
    NKJV: *charge*

Esther

1. NIV; NKJV: *furious*
   KJV: *wroth*

2. NIV: *discord*

3. NIV: also *decree*
   KJV: also *commandment*
   NKJV: *decree*

4. KJV: *writing*
   NKJV: *document*

5. NIV: *issued*
   KJV; NKJV: *written*

6. NIV: also *annihilation*
   KJV: *destroy*
   NKJV: also *destroy*

7. NIV: also *order*

8. NIV: *overruling*
   KJV: *reverse*

NOTES FOR PERSONAL STUDY

NOTES FOR PERSONAL STUDY

NOTES FOR PERSONAL STUDY

NOTES FOR PERSONAL STUDY

BOOKS IN THE
NEW INDUCTIVE STUDY SERIES

Teach Me Your Ways
Genesis, Exodus,
Leviticus, Numbers,
Deuteronomy

Choosing Victory,
Overcoming Defeat
Joshua, Judges, Ruth

Desiring God's Own Heart
1 & 2 Samuel,
1 Chronicles

Come Walk in My Ways
1 & 2 Kings, 2 Chronicles

Overcoming Fear and
Discouragement
Ezra, Nehemiah, Esther

God's Blueprint for
Bible Prophecy
Daniel

The Call to Follow Jesus
Luke

The Holy Spirit
Unleashed in You
Acts

God's Answers for
Relationships and Passions
1 & 2 Corinthians

Free from Bondage
God's Way
Galatians, Ephesians

That I May Know Him
Philippians, Colossians

Standing Firm in
These Last Days
1 & 2 Thessalonians

Walking in Power, Love,
and Discipline
1 & 2 Timothy, Titus

Living with Discernment
in the End Times
1 & 2 Peter, Jude

Behold, Jesus Is Coming!
Revelation

HARVEST HOUSE BOOKS
BY KAY ARTHUR

જ્જ્જ્જ

Beloved
God, Are You There?
How to Study Your Bible
Israel, My Beloved (A Novel)
Lord, Teach Me to Pray in 28 Days
A Marriage Without Regrets
A Marriage Without Regrets Study Guide
A Moment with God
My Savior, My Friend
Speak to My Heart, God
With an Everlasting Love (A Novel)

Discover 4 Yourself
Inductive Bible Studies for Kids

How to Study Your Bible for Kids
God's Amazing Creation (Genesis 1–2)
Digging Up the Past (Genesis 3–11)
Joseph—God's Superhero (Genesis 37–50)
Wrong Way, Jonah! (Jonah)
Jesus in the Spotlight (John 1–11)
Jesus—Awesome Power, Awesome Love (John 11–16)
Jesus—To Eternity and Beyond! (John 17–21)
Boy, Have I Got Problems! (James)
Lord, Teach Me to Pray for Kids

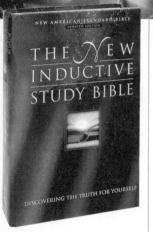

DIGGING DEEPER

Books in the New Inductive Study Series are survey courses. If you want to do a more in-depth study of a particular book of the Bible, we suggest that you do a Precept Upon Precept Bible Study Course on that book. The Precept studies require approximately five hours of personal study a week. You may obtain more information on these powerful courses by contacting Precept Ministries International at 800-763-8280, visiting our website at www.precept.org, or filling out and mailing the response card in the back of this book.

If you desire to expand and sharpen your skills, you would really benefit by attending a Precept Ministries Institute of Training. The Institutes are conducted throughout the United States, Canada, and in a number of other countries. Class lengths vary from one to five days, depending on the course you are interested in. For more information on the Precept Ministries Institute of Training, call Precept Ministries.